THE QUMRAN BAPTISM AND JOHN THE BAPTIST'S BAPTISM

Leonard F. Badia

University Press of America

Library of Congress Catalog Card Number: 80-5438

To the memory of

my gentle and loving father

who loved knowledge

PREFACE

The purpose of this work is to present an examination and
critical evaluation of the Qumranian "Baptism" and John the
Baptist's Baptism.

Since the discovery of the Dead Sea Scrolls in 1947,
scholars have speculated about John the Baptist being a member
of the Qumran Community or at least influenced by their "baptism"
rite.

These pages contain a detailed study of this problem. I
hope my work will add some light in the search for the truth.

Chapter one examines the historical background of the
Qumran Community: their identification, geographic location,
time of occupation and the reason for their occupation. It
also examines the identity of John the Baptist, the geographic
location of his ministry, and his possible contact with Qumran.

Chapter two explores the Qumranian "Baptism" which is
mentioned in their Manual of Discipline scroll. In this section
five areas are considered: 1) archaeological evidence of
cisterns and basins, 2) interpretation of terms--Ablution,
Lustration, and Baptism, 3) a comparison of William Brownlee's
and Geza Vermes' translation of the Manual of Discipline scroll,
4) various biblical scholars opinions about the Qumranian
"Baptism", 5) a summary.

Chapter three examines John the Baptist's Baptism which
is mentioned in the Synoptic Gospels. Five areas are considered:
1) identification of the Synoptic Gospels, 2) interpretation of
terms--Rite, Sacrament, and Baptism, 3) a comparison of the
Revised Standard Version and the Jerusalem Bible Version of the
Synoptic Gospels, 4) various biblical scholars opinions about
John's baptism, 5) a summary.

Chapter four summarizes the comparisons between the
Qumranian "Baptism" and John the Baptist's Baptism. Finally,
several conclusions are made.

Rev. Leonard F. Badia, Ph.D.
St. John's University, New York

v

CONTENTS

INTRODUCTION

It was during the spring of 1947. One of the greatest archaeological discoveries of this mid century was made purely by accident. Three Bedouin shepherds discovered clay jars containing scrolls which were destined to create what would be called a new era of Biblical studies in the western world. The discovery was made in a cave secluded among the rocky crags that overlook the northwest shore of the Dead Sea in present day Israel. The tribesmen attempted to sell the scrolls to antiquity dealers in Bethlehem. Ultimately, four scrolls came into the hands of the Syrian Patriarch of Jerusalem, Mar Athanasius Yeshue Samuel. Three other scrolls were purchased by Professor E. L. Sukenik for the Hebrew University of Jerusalem. The scrolls of the Patriarch were identified as ancient by scholars of the American School of Oriental Research in Jerusalem. Within a short time, Professor Sukenik reached the same conclusion. Eventually all these scrolls were purchased by the State of Israel in 1954 and are now displayed in the building called the Shrine of the Book. Since 1951 the exploration of the area has revealed other scrolls and thousands of fragments.

From a biblical point of view, the value of the Dead Sea Scrolls has already proved to be tremendous. The fact that Biblical Hebrew manuscripts copied before the tenth century A.D. have at last been discovered, is a monumental value. It is estimated that more than 125 Old Testament manuscripts, representing every book except Esther have been discovered in the Qumran caves. Some are more than a thousand years older than previously known documents in Biblical Hebrew. A whole new horizon for Biblical textual studies has dawned.

The scholar cannot assume that the greater age of these documents guarantees their textual superiority. Each point must be weighed carefully, and many variant readings in them may be rejected on sound grounds. Others will be disputed. Nevertheless, the Qumran scrolls have provided scholars with a major breakthrough into the complex prehistory of the standard Hebrew text of the Old Testament. For the layman, on the other hand, these documents give new information about religious Jews of the first century A.D., John the Baptist and Jesus.

CHAPTER 1

THE HISTORICAL BACKGROUND OF QUMRAN AND JOHN THE BAPTIST

A. QUMRAN

The Qumran community was composed of Jews who considered themselves as the elect remnant of Israel, who would emerge in the last days from the purging judgment of God. In order to prepare for this judgment, they advocated a renewal of the covenant of Moses by a strict repentance and a new obedience to the requirements of the covenant. Naturally, this greatly influenced their lives.

Identification of the Qumran Sect

There is no certainty as to what the members of the Qumran sect called themselves. The term, Qumran, has been ascribed to them by contemporary scholars. However, some scholars referred to them as Zealots, Pharisees, Sadducees and Essenes. Among the authorities concerned with this problem are Cecil Roth[1] and Geoffrey Driver,[2] who believe they were Zealots. The Zealots, who were opposed by some Pharisees according to Finkelstein,[3] rejected all compromise with Rome and acknowledged only God as the ruler of Palestine. Russell says of the Zealots, "It is wrong to regard them simply as a radical group within the state who stirred up trouble with the Romans . . . they were essentially a company of Jewish patriots motivated by deep religious convictions."[4] On the other hand, Bright thinks the Zealots were "fanatically brave and reckless men who were ready to strike for independence regardless of the odds."[5] However, Pryke[6] and other scholars do not share Roth's and Driver's hypothesis because it does not support the literary, archaeological, and palaeographical evidence found at Qumran.

Burrows[7] agrees with some scholars that it is highly improbable Qumran was a Pharisaic community. Yet, Davies[8] believes some Pharisees may have been in Qumran but it is most unlikely that they comprised a very large segment of the population.

1

Finally, could the people at Qumran be Essenes? And, if so, were the Essenes, as described in the writings of Josephus, Philo, and Pliny the Elder, the same people who settled at Qumran (4 B.C. - 68 A.D.). Most scholars accept the theory that the Qumranians were a branch of the Essene movement.

Although many scholars have presented considerable evidence in support of the Essene theory, it is not a proved fact; yet it is the soundest theory. In order to avoid confusion, I refer to the people of Qumran as Qumranians.

Geographic Location of Qumran

The site of Qumran may be the ancient salt city, the valley of Anchor, the site of Secacah, or none of these.[9] Khirbet Qumran is the name of the site that lies approximately four to ten miles south of Jericho in Palestine.[10] The etymology of the word Qumran is obscure. It is called Khirbet by the Arabs meaning a hill with ruins on it or for ruins alone.[11] The area of Qumran has been called the Wilderness.[12]

The meaning of wilderness is questioned. The Hebrew word "midbar" means pasturage, wilderness, steppe,[13] or frequently a defined tract of wilderness or the wilderness of a particular region.[14] The Hebrew word "midbar" also means grazing land and the Greek word "Eremos" means a lonely, uncultivated, uninhabited place.[15]

Burrows expresses skepticism about the meaning of wilderness; others claim that it was nothing more than a non-local expression in Near East mythologies. Yet, geological and meterological data seem to justify its meaning as the wilderness of Sinai or the wilderness of Judea.[16] In any case, the wilderness was a natural place for those who were dissatisfied with existing conditions as well as for those who wished a rendezvous place relatively free of detection. Whether it is accepted in the wider or the narrower sense of the word, the wilderness of Judea is the activity area of the Qumran people.[17]

Time of Occupation

Archaeology shows there were three main periods of occupation

of the Qumran site, as follows: the first quarter of the first
century, B.C., or earlier to 31 B.C. when a severe earthquake
shook Judea; 4 B.C. to June 68 A.D. when the Roman army under
Vespasian destroyed it; 132-135 A.D. during the short-lived
second Jewish revolt.[18] However, it is the second occupation of
the area of Qumran (4 B.C. - 68 A.D.) which concerns us.

Reason for Occupation

The conditions of Palestine in the first century A.D. were
not stable. According to Roth,[19] the Romans were not in complete
military control of the country but were a great menace to the
Palestinian Jew. Both politically and religiously, the Jewish
priests were the authorities during the first century A.D. when
the Judaean area of Palestine was in perpetual fever of religious
excitement. Finkelstein[20] says it was inevitable that there would
be a clash between Rome and Palestine. Rome avoided internal
interference as much as possible; however, the Roman procurators
of Judaea were mostly irresponsible men. Whether some Jews went
to Qumran from different areas of Palestine for political,
military, or strictly religious motives, or a combination of these
motives is not certain, but it seems to have been primarily for
religious motives.[21]

B. JOHN THE BAPTIST

The main source of material concerning John the Baptist is
the New Testament. In the New Testament, the fullest accounts
are found in Matthew, Mark and Luke. The material is not
extensive, but one is able to sketch the life and ministry of
John from it. Of all the people who are mentioned in the New
Testament, none seems likely to have had a closer connection with
the Qumran community than John the Baptist. Millar Burrows
said, "There is no reason why one should be so reluctant to
believe that John was or had been a member of their community.
The only question is whether there is good reason to suppose
that he was, or that he had anything to do with the sect.[22]

Identification of John the Baptist

The Synoptic Gospels are a source of material concerning

John the Baptist. The material is not extensive, but it is possible to form a sketch of his life and ministry from it.

John was the son of Zechariah, the priest (Luke 1:5), and he was born about six months before Jesus. (Luke 1:36) His parents were advanced in years. (Luke 1:7) About his childhood, Luke says, "And the child grew and became strong in spirit, and he was in the wilderness till the day of his manifestation to Israel." (Luke 1:80) Luke alludes to his vocation, saying, "In the fifteenth year of the reign of Tiberias Caesar, Pontius Pilate being governor of Judea, and Herod being the tetrarch of Galilee, and his brother, Philip, tetrarch of the region of Ituraea and Trachonitis, and Lysanias tetrarch of Abilene in the high-priesthood of Annas and Caiaphas, the word of God came to John the son of Zechariah in the wilderness." (Luke 3:1-2)

Although Luke's gospel gives an account of John's birth and early childhood, Matthew and Mark are silent on these points. Their information about his death is sparse. Matthew says, "Now when John heard in prison about the deeds of the Christ, he sent word by his disciples." (Matthew 11:2) This led to later reference on the part of Jesus to John as the greatest of prophets. In Mark's writing, it states that John was beheaded on the order of King Herod. (Mark 6:14-29) The picture of John in the Synoptic Gospels is consistent and there seems to be no contradictory material in them. As far as the time of his death, the Synoptic Gospels do not give an exact date, but an approximation. It was during the reign of Herod the Great's sons, Philip, Archelaus and Antipas.[23] Some scholars believe his death occurred during the reign of Herod Antipas who was exiled approximately 39 or 40 A.D.[24] LaSor[25] says, according to Luke's account, John began his public ministry approximately at the age of thirty, which was about 27 or 28 A.D. His ministry did not last long, perhaps six months, since Herod Antipas had him beheaded at Machaerus in the spring of 28 A.D.[26] Driver[27] believes that John was beheaded around 28-30 A.D. by order of Herod Archelaus. Another report claims that he was beheaded in the spring of 29 A.D. by Herod Antipas.[28] It seems certain John was killed by one of Herod the Great's sons and that it happened before 40 A.D. Thus, John the Baptist was a contemporary of the Qumran community.

Geographic Location of John's Ministry

The ministry of John is reported in all three gospel accounts. Luke says, "In the high priesthood of Annas and Caiaphas, the word of God came to John the son of Zechariah in the wilderness; and he went into all the region about the Jordan, preaching a baptism of repentance for the forgiveness of sins." (Luke 3:2-3) In Matthew's account, it says, "In those days came John the Baptist, preaching in the wilderness of Judea, Repent for the kingdom of heaven is at hand." (Matthew 3:1-2) He further states, "Jesus came from Galilee to the Jordan to John, to be baptized by him." (Matthew 3:13) According to Mark, "John appeared in the wilderness, preaching a baptism of repentance for the forgiveness of sins" (Mark 1:4) and "In those days Jesus came from Nazareth of Galilee and was baptized by John in the Jordan." (Mark 1:9) From these passages it may be concluded that John conducted his ministry in the wilderness at or near the river Jordan. The problem is what does the wilderness mean and what is the precise location of the river Jordan?

The term "wilderness" might mean the desert of Judah, which is the area of the Dead Sea and the valley of the Jordan.[29] Fernandez[30] and Prat[31] say that it refers to the desert of Juda, the arid and sparsely cultivated territory that extends east from the mountains of Judea, or, in other words, from Jerusalem to Bethlehem. Some scholars[32] claim that it means the desert of Judea, west of the Jordan and the Dead Sea, near Jericho. McKenzie[33] says that it is the steep slope that falls from the central ridge of the country to the valley of the Jordan and the Dead Sea. In the widest term, wilderness was applied to the Negev, the desert that comprises the southern half of Israel. The word, "wilderness", according to McCown, really means a lonely, uncultivated, uninhabited place but not necessarily deprived of water.[34] It could also mean a grazing land or steppe but it almost never applied to the Jordan valley. It, perhaps included the western bank of the Jordan to the north of the Dead Sea.[35] In general, the term "wilderness" means regions or districts that were not cultivated, and it could, therefore, refer to the area between the valley of the Jordan and the Arabah.[36] The Hebrew word, midbar, means an uninhabited, uncultivated land and sometimes signifies a pasturage for flocks.[37] Brownlee[38] says that the wilderness of Judea means the hot, desolate hills along the west bank of the Dead Sea. Therefore, John's ministry was conducted in the wilderness of Judea, probably the area lying between the Judaean plateau on the West and the lower area of the Jordan and the Dead Sea to the East.

Just as it is difficult to determine the exact meaning of wilderness in the Synoptic Gospels, so also it is difficult to specify the term Jordan. In the Synoptics, it states that John the Baptist preached in the region near the Jordan and that Jesus was baptized by him in the river Jordan. Again, the problem is exactly where did John preach in the Jordan valley and baptize in the Jordan river? Steinmueller[39] says that the river Jordan flows from north to south through the great rift that extends through southern Syria into the Jordan valley. It runs between the lake of Galilee and the Dead Sea, a distance of sixty-five miles. About eight miles north of the Dead Sea, on the west side stood the city of Jericho in the Jordan valley. It is interesting to note that the Jordan river comes to an end in the Dead Sea, which is approximately fifty miles long and ten miles wide. As the Jordan approaches the Dead Sea, the valley widens and there are many springs and there is vegetation. Its average width from the Sea of Galilee to the Dead Sea is ninety to one-hundred feet and its depth three to ten feet. During the time of John the Baptist, cities such as Phasaelis, Bethannabris, Abila, Livias, and Rameh existed in the Jordan Valley, and it is easy to understand how many people came from the region about the Jordan to hear the preaching of John. Therefore, John's baptismal ministry was almost certainly close to the fords of the Jordan near Jericho, which is less than ten miles from Qumran.

Possible Contact with Qumran

Since the Synoptic Gospels say that John preached and baptized in the valley of the Jordan, and Qumran is in the vicinity of the Jordan valley, it has been alleged by Danielou that John shared the Qumranian life or was in contact with it.[40] It has brought up the question whether John was a member of the Qumran community or at least knew about its members, or possibly came into contact with them and was influenced by their teachings and rituals.

Driver[41] mentions that John was born either in Ain Karim or a nearby village, twenty miles from Qumran. Other scholars[42] also share this point of view. From the synoptic accounts, it is learned that John was the son of a priest. Cullman,[43] Steinman,[44] Danielou,[45] and LaSor[46] agree that he was a priest's son. From the translated Manual of Discipline scroll, it is known that the Qumranian community was composed of some priests and was partially ruled by them. Therefore it is possible that John, being a priest's

6

son, would have been welcomed by them if he went to Qumran or he
would at least feel favorably disposed toward them. Like the
Qumranians, he was a deeply religious person who was committed to
the laws of God and to call men to repentance.

In addition to John's being a priest's son, Jesus calls him
a prophet. (Luke 7:26) Also, scholars have called John a prophet.
For example, Conzelman[47] calls him the last of the prophets;
Dupont-Sommer[48] refers to him as an independent prophet; [50]
Robinson[49] says that he was an individual prophet; Pryke[50] says
that he was an ascetical prophet, and Bruce[51] simply calls him
a prophet. The Hebrew word nabi, the usual word for prophet,
means "to call," or "speak aloud." Therefore, it seems reasonable to say that John was a prophet.

So far, several points have been considered: namely, John's
birthplace, his being a priest's son, and being called a prophet.
Now, the opinions of various scholars on whether or not John
was a member of the Qumran community will be examined. I believe
that Harrison,[52] Scobie,[53] Robinson[54] and Cullman[55] make the
reasonable assumption that John was not a member of the Qumran
community but was in contact with the Qumranians, since his
ministry was in the locality of Qumran. The Qumran writings
reveal that they lived in the wilderness of Judea. Likewise, the
Synoptic Gospels record that John preached and baptized in the
wilderness of Judea. The child John the Baptist was "in the
desert" until he began his public ministry. (Luke 1:80; 3:23)
John was born of a priestly family (Luke 1:5) which would have
made him acceptable to the Qumran community which was priestly in
origin. John's mission was a message of repentance, which was
similar to the Qumran message of repentance. Finally, John the
Baptist's ministry was at or near the Jordan river, which was in
the vicinity of the Qumran community.

On the other hand, there are many scholars who are not sure
if John was a member of the Qumran community, but who believe he
may have been in contact with the Qumranians. Allegro[56] says
John may have been adopted by the community when his father died.
It is not improbable that he spent his childhood in the wilderness and was influenced by the Qumran community.[57] Mowry[58] agrees
with Brownlee.

However, the present translated material from Qumran provides
no proof that John was reared at Qumran. Because of the nature

7

of the community, it would be a weak assumption to hold that he was a member. Still, because of John's ministry in the wilderness and the Jordan Valley, Schubert[59] believes John may have held temporary membership in the Qumran. Again, because John and the Qumranians lived in the same general area, Danielou,[60] Steinmann,[61] Finnegan,[62] and Brown[63] believe John had to have some contact with the Qumran community. Even if he had come into contact with them, Rowley[64] says he did not borrow anything from their baptismal rite. Heron[65] differs with Rowley and he shows the similarity between John's repentance idea and the Qumran baptism, which demanded the notion of repentance.

Fritsch,[66] however, believes that John was a member of the Qumran community. According to Burrows,[67] there is no reason why one should be reluctant to believe that John was, or had been, a member.

Some scholars are very cautious in their statements about John's possible contact with Qumran. Benoit[68] and Cross[69] say that some connection existed between John and Qumran. Gordon[70] and Sutcliffe[71] state that John lived in the same area of Qumran. This is a reasonable assumption since the Matthew gospel records, "In those days came John the Baptist, preaching in the wilderness of Judea" (3:1-2) and "then went out to him Jerusalem and all Judea and the region about the Jordan and they were baptized by him in the river Jordan confessing their sins." (3:5-6) Finally, Stauffer[72] says that Qumran was the "spiritual home of John the Baptist." Although there is no consensus among the scholars that John was a member of the Qumran community, it is reasonable to assume that he was a contemporary of the Qumranians and that he preached and baptized in the general vicinity of Qumran.

CHAPTER 2

THE QUMRAN BAPTISM

Having examined the historical background of the Qumran
community and John the Baptist, let us look at the Qumran
"Baptism."

Perhaps the most distinctive development that took place
within the Qumran community was the great emphasis the people
placed on their ablutions, lustrations, or "baptisms." Judging
from this, it seems that purification was of paramount con-
sideration for the Qumranians. The laws of purity and impurity
were expressed for them in Leviticus (Chapters 11-17), Numbers
(Chapter 19) and Deuteronomy (Chapter 14), the Third, Fourth,
and Fifth Books of the Torah, respectively. In these books,
four sources of impurity are apparent: leprosy, issues from
human sexual organs, the dead bodies of certain animals, and
particularly human corpses. Man could be defiled by impure
things. For the Qumranians, like many of their Jewish contemporaries, water became the principal method of purification.[2] In
the Old Testament, water sometimes represented the instrument
(Genesis 7:11 ff.) or the symbol (Isaiah 43:2) of destruction or
danger. It also could be the instrument or symbol of blessing
(Zechariah 14:8), the instrument of cleansing (Numbers 19:7;
Leviticus 14:8), or the symbol of cleansing from iniquity (Isaiah
1:16; Ezechial 36:25). Therefore, water could correct the state
of impurity; after the ablutions, the person or object became
pure once more. He remained in the pure state until impurity was
contracted again.

Usually, the only cleansing a person received from water
was external, a physical purity.[73] It fulfilled the laws of
purity that enabled a person to be admitted once again to religious
ceremonies.[74] For example, water in the form of baths, was prescribed in the book of Leviticus; one had to bathe after being
cured of leprosy (Leviticus 14:8-9) and after contracting personal
uncleanliness (Leviticus 15, 11, 13, 16, 18). These ritual baths
(Hebrew-Telilah) became increasingly important during the Second
Temple Period (500 B.C. - 70 A.D.).[75]

Both Brownlee's and Vermes' translations of the Manual of
Discipline (3:4-9; 5:13-14) indicate that the Qumran washings were
not just ceremonial, ritual or physical washings, but were re-
garded as meaningless if they were not accompanied by a genuine
internal repentance.[76] Hence, Ringgren,[77] Vermes,[78] Sutcliffe,[79]
and Cross[80] say that Qumran washings were both a physical and
moral purification, and a person could not achieve one without
the other.

ARCHAEOLOGICAL EVIDENCE

From the Manual of Discipline, it is clear that "baptisms"
were prescribed for purification. Archaeological evidence shows
that there were elaborate cisterns and basins to supply large
amounts of water to the community. De Vaux,[81] the archaeologist,
made the following observations: 1) All cisterns except two, not
counting the basins attached to them, are equipped with a large
flight of steps descending into them. The upper steps are divided
by low partitions, which form several parallel descents. Caution
must be exercised in accepting the belief that these cisterns may
have been used for ritual baths, because similar cisterns in the
same period and in the same area have been discovered that
definitely did not have a ritualistic function; 2) The Qumran
cisterns were probably merely cisterns; 3) There are, however,
two small basins with flights of steps and these are certainly
baths, but it is impossible to determine whether the baths had
a ritual significance.

Brownlee[82] states that it is the nature of the community
rather than the distinctiveness of the cisterns themselves that
makes it probable that some of them may have served as bathing
pools. One of these cisterns, he says, was constructed indoors,
which lends credence to the bathing theory.

Like De Vaux, Cross,[83] and Sutcliffe[84] believe that the
cisterns were places for the storage of water during the rainy
season of winter and early spring. The summer months were
practically rainless so that a good supply of water was required
for the needs of the community. Both Milik[85] and Driver[86] agree
that the water system, with its aqueducts and canals, was linked
together, but it is unknown for what purposes the tanks, cisterns
and communal basins were used. Fritsch[87] states that the different
arrangements and grouping of steps indicated that they were used

for baptismal or ablution rites. According to Cross,[88] if the Qumranians practiced a ritual baptism, they probably would have used the Jordan River or the waters of Ain Feshkha near Qumran instead of the waters from the cisterns or basins. Allegro[89] suggests that at least two of the cisterns are of a size and shape consistent with their use as baptistries. Two of these cisterns are different from the usual Roman type of cistern, says Ringgren;[90] he believes they were used for minor lustrations. Finally, Gordon[91] simply states that "baptismal pools have been unearthed at Khirbet Qumran."

Hence, although archaeology has established that there were cisterns, basins and a large water supply system at Qumran, the purposes for which these cisterns and basins were used cannot be logically deduced from the data. What seems clear at this point is that it is not certain the water supply was used for ceremonial purposes; it is also uncertain whether the basins had a function different from that of the cisterns.

INTERPRETATION OF TERMS--ABLUTION, LUSTRATION, AND BAPTISM

Scholars use the terms ablution, lustrations or baptism to describe the washings that took place at Qumran. Briefly, let us examine the meaning of these words.

In Hebrew, ablution means immersion, the act of washing performed to correct a condition of ritual impurity, and restore one to a state of ritual purity.[92] Ablutions must not be associated only with ritual washings for the sake of cleanliness. At Qumran, these ablutions also were symbolic of moral purity.[93] The latter depended on the interior disposition of the person.[94] Thus, the clothing of a leper (Leviticus 13, 6, 34, 54-48), one who had been in a leper's house (Leviticus 14, 47), and the house itself (Leviticus 14, 52) were to be washed.

Washing also removed the polution resulting from sexual intercourse. When Jeremiah, the prophet, described the sinfulness of Israel, he said, "though you wash yourself with lye and use much soap, the stain of your guilt is still before me, says the Lord God" (Jeremiah 2:22). The sins of the nation would still not be removed. Although these examples in the book of Leviticus point to the need for ritual purity as well as moral purity, the Manual of Discipline (3:4-9) of the Qumranians also alludes to it.

In Jewish tradition, there were three types of ablutions according to the type of impurity contracted: complete immersion of the whole body, immersion of the hands and feet, and immersion of hands only.[95] These ablutions were usually performed in a stream, spring, river, or a mikveh.[96] The Mikveh[97] was a pool or bath of clear natural water in which a person immersed himself in order to become ritually pure. However, if the person were repentant of his faults, it would cleanse him morally as well as ritually.[98] It seems clear that purification by water was necessary either by bath, as in a mikveh, or a simple ablution, even prior to 70 A.D.[99] For example, washing of the entire body was necessary if a person came into contact with an unclean person or with things that belonged to this person (Leviticus 15:5-10). At the installation of priests, it was required that the entire body be washed (Exodus 24:4).

From the book of Leviticus, it is clear that there were several types of washing. The object could be plunged into water (Leviticus 11:32), or the person led to the water (Leviticus 14:7), or the person washed in running water (Leviticus 14:13).

Some scholars, such as Cross.[100] refer to the washings at Qumran as lustrations. By this is meant a formal and public application of water in token of consecration or expiation.[101] For the ancient Greeks, Romans, and Jews, on solemn occasions it usually took the form of sprinkling of water.

The question arises as to what scholars mean precisely by the term lustration. Although Cross[102] uses the term, lustrations, he does not specify whether he means a sprinkling of water or a bath. Sutcliffe,[103] who also uses the term, means bathing.

Finally, there is the third term, baptism, used by some scholars like Black[104] and Larson,[105] to describe the washings at Qumran. If the word baptism is being used to signify the washing ceremonies at Qumran, then it must be understood in the Jewish sense of the word and not the Christian. According to the Jews, baptism means a religious ablution signifying purification or consecration.[106] In the Christian sense of the word, baptism means "to dip in" or "under" water as an initiatory rite into a specific group or community.[107] However, it is still disputed among authorities of Judaism whether baptism was practiced as an initiatory rite to Judaism prior to the destruction of the Temple in 70 A.D.[108]

It seems that many scholars avoid the term, baptism, when they refer to the washings at Qumran. Perhaps they do so because the term may be misunderstood to mean Christian baptism. Scholars seem to favor either the term lustrations or ablutions. Neither Brownlee nor Vermes use the term, baptism, in their translations of the Manual of Discipline. In fact, Vermes uses the term ablutions (3:4-5), whereas Brownlee uses the term washings in his translation (3:4-5) Both men, however, clearly mean that the Qumranian washings (ablutions) were moral washings.

COMPARISON OF BROWNLEE'S AND VERMES' TRANSLATION OF THE MANUAL OF DISCIPLINE

The moral washings of the Qumranians are mentioned in three passages of the Manual of Discipline.

The first passage of the Manual of Discipline (3:4-9) seems to lay down the conditions necessary for admittance to and continuance in the community that demanded purification. Apparently, the Qumranians demanded several conditions for membership of which two were basic for purification. First, there was the water cleansing (3:4-5). Second, there was the further need for moral purification, that is, the observance of the Laws of God (3:6). In order to achieve this moral purification, the person had to have a proper interior disposition (3:8-9).

For clarity, I have divided the first passage (3:4-9) according to the various aspects discussed in the Manual of Discipline document.

Man's Purification Is Not Accomplished
Just by Water Itself

The translations (3:4-5) of both Vermes and Brownlee are very similar with slight differences. For example, they indicate it is water that is used for ablutions, however, something more is required for purification. Their difference lies in the word "himself." Brownlee indicates that the ablution was self-administered, saying, "nor cleanse himself with any water for washing" (3:5). Vermes omits the word himself.

Brownlee	Vermes
He can not purify himself by atonement, nor cleanse with water for impurity, nor sanctify himself with seas or rivers, nor cleanse himself with any water for washing.(3:4-5)	He shall neither be purified by atonement, nor cleansed by purifying waters, nor sanctified by seas and rivers, nor washed clean with any ablution. (3:4-5)

Man's Purification Depends on the Observance of God's Law

From their translation (3:6), it seems clear that a person was considered unclean as long as he rejected the ordinances of God. A moral purification seems to be required.

Brownlee	Vermes
Unclean! Unclean! shall he be as long as he rejects God's laws. (3:6)	Unclean, unclean shall he be. For as long as he despises the precepts of God. (3:6)

Man's Impurity Excluded Him from the Community's Counsel

Both translations of the passage (3:6) indicate that the impure man will not be instructed by the community until he repents. Brownlee and Vermes use the identical term, Community of His Counsel, in their translations. Apparently, the neophyte or the lapsed member was subject strictly to the rules of the community.

Brownlee	Vermes
For it is through the spirit of God's true counsel in regard to a man's ways that all his iniquities will be atoned. (3:6-7)	For it is through the spirit of true counsel concerning the ways of man that all his sins shall be expiated. (3:6-7)

There Were Conditions for Man's Forgiveness

Basically, Brownlee's and Vermes' translations of the passage about the conditions for man's forgiveness are the same. In summarizing this passage, one can reduce the moral conditions required for the Qumranian baptism to genuine repentance and amendment of one's ways.

Brownlee	Vermes
Through an upright and humble spirit that his sin till be atoned, and through the submission of his soul to all God's ordinances that his flesh will be cleansed. (3:8-9)	He shall be cleansed from all his sins by the spirit of holiness uniting him to His truth, and his iniquity shall be expiated by the spirit of uprightness and humility. (3:8-9)

The Fulfillment of the Moral Conditions and Physical Washing Will Atone for All Sins

The slight variance in translations of this passage (3:8) is not significant. It seems that the Qumranians did not place a limitation on the number or type of sins that could be forgiven if they observed the moral and physical conditions. The two translations say the same thing that all their sins would be forgiven if they observed certain conditions.

Brownlee	Vermes
That he will be cleansed of all iniquities. (3:8)	He shall be cleansed from all sins. (3:8)

Water Is Used in the Qumranian Moral Washing

Both translations state clearly that water was used by the Qumranians for their purification rite. However, Brownlee describes the water as rippling water, while Vermes says that it was cleansing water. From Brownlee's translation it seems that the Qumranian washing could have taken place in a stream or river where the waters are in constant motion. At least, it seems to be a possibility that these baptisms were performed in a stream or river rather than in a basin or cistern. On the other hand, Vermes' translation indicates that the Qumranian purification rite was done by sprinkling the person with cleansing water. Therefore, it seems that water was set aside for a purification rite. This water could have been the water in the basins or cisterns in the Qumran settlement. Vermes adds the point of sprinkling. If Vermes is correct, the question arises

whether the Qumranians were speaking in a figurative or literal
manner. Likewise, the same question can be asked about Brownlee's
translation, rippling water. What seems certain is that the
Qumranians used water for their purification rite. The place of
the water purification rite cannot be deduced from the translation of this passage. Similarly, it cannot be determined how
the moral washing was done.

Brownlee	Vermes
So that he may purify himself with water for impurity and sanctify himself with rippling water. (3:9)	And when his flesh is sprinkled with purifying water and sanctified by cleansing water. (3:9)

In another section of the <u>Manual of Discipline</u> (5:13-14),
there is a reference to the purification rites of the
Qumranians. It seems to refer to the need of repentance before
an unclean person could associate with the purified members of
the Qumran community. The two translations of this passage do
not indicate whether it applies to the neophyte or the lapsed
member of the community or both. Unlike the first section of
the <u>Manual of Discipline</u> (3:4-9) Brownlee's and Vermes' translations of another section of the <u>Manual of Discipline</u> (5:13-14)
are notably different. First, Vermes' translation indicates
that the unclean person could not eat the Pure Meal unless he
was first purified. Borwnlee's translation says nothing about
the Pure Meal. He states that the unclean person could not touch
the Purity of the Holy Men until he was purified. Second, each
translator calls the full-fledged members different names.
Vermes calls them Saints, while Brownlee refers to them as Holy
Men. Obviously, the main difference seems to be Vermes' translation as Pure Meal and Brownlee's translation as purity. In
either case, it is apparent that the unclean person, the neophyte
or the lapsed member could not associate with the pure (morally
and physically clean) full-fledged member of the community.

Brownlee	Vermes
These may not enter into water to be permitted to touch the Purity of the holy men, for they will not be cleansed unless they have turned from their	They shall not enter the water to partake of the pure Meal of the saints, for they shall not be cleansed unless they turn from their wickedness: for all who

wickedness, for uncleanness   transgress His word are unclean.
clings to all transgressors
of His word (5:13-14)

The third section of the Manual of Discipline (6:14-23)
seems to refer to the requirement for admission into the community. These requirements apparently were: 1) Membership was
restricted to Jews (6:14). 2) There was an examination of the
neophyte by an Overseer or Guardian (6:14). 3) The neophyte was
informed about the life of the community (6:14). 4) There was
an unspecified probation period prior to his temporary admittance
into the community (6:15-16). 5) There was another examination of the neophyte and an admittance decision had to be
made by the whole community (6:15-16). 6) There was a one-
year probation before the neophyte could be admitted to the
Purity of the Many (6:16-17). 7) At the completion of the second
year of probation, the neophyte was admitted to the Drink of the
Many (6:20-21). 8) After the completion of the second year and
another examination, the neophyte was permanently admitted into
the community. (6:21-22).

A comparison of Brownlee's and Vermes' translation of this
passage of the Manual of Discipline (6:14-23) reveals great
similarities. However, although their translations are basically
similar, there are variations. For example, Vermes uses expressions such as "Pure Meal," "Drink of the Congregation,"
"Saints," and "Guardian." On the other hand, Brownlee uses
expressions such as "Many," "Drink of the Many," "Purity of the
Many," and "Overseer," which are not found in Vermes' translation.

Brownlee	Vermes
And everyone from Israel who dedicates himself to join the Council of the Community.(6:14)	Every man, born of Israel, who freely pledges himself to join the Council of the Community. (6:14)
The man who is Overseer at the head of the Many shall examine him as to his understanding and his deeds. (6:14)	. . . shall be examined by the Guardian at the head of the Con-gregation concerning his under-standing and his deeds. (6:14)
And if he grasps instruction, he shall bring him into the cove-	If he is fitted to the discipline, he shall admit him into the

17

nant to turn to the truth and to turn away from all perversity. (6:14-15)

covenant that he may be converted to the truth and depart from all falsehood. (6:14-15)

The whole group will be asked concerning his affairs; and however it is decided under God in accordance with the counsel of the Many, he will either draw near or draw away. (6:15-16)

When he comes to stand before the Congregation, they shall all deliberate his case, and according to the decision of the Council of the Congregation he shall either enter or depart. (6:15-16)

He must not touch the Purity of the Many until they investigate him as to his spirit and his deeds, until the completion of a full year by him. (6:16-17)

He shall not touch the pure Meal of the Congregation until one full year is completed. (6:16-17)

He, the neophyte, shall not touch the drink of the Many until the completion of a second year among the men of the Community. (6:20-21)

He shall not touch the Drink of the Congregation until he has completed a second year among the men of the Community. (6:20-21)

But upon his completion of a second year, he, the Overseer, shall examine him under the direction of the Many, and if it is decided under God to admit him into the Community, he shall enroll him. (6:21-22)

But when the second year has passed, he shall be examined, and if it be his destiny according to the judgement of the Congregation to enter the Community, then shall be inscribed among his brethen. (6:21-22)

In conclusion, the comparison of Brownlee's and Vermes' translations of these three passages of the Manual of Discipline shows that they are quite similar.

BIBLICAL SCHOLARS OPINIONS

Because of Brownlee's and Vermes' translation of the Manual of Discipline scroll which contains the Qumranian moral washings, scholars have voiced opinions about these moral washings.

Scholars have interpreted these passages in the <u>Manual of Discipline</u> in various ways. For purposes of clarity, I have grouped these findings under eight headings.

1. The Qumran Washings Are Lustrations or Ablutions with or without Requirement of Repentance

Fritsch[109] says that the Qumran washings were a purification rite before the common meal. Neither the candidate's atonement nor the water could purify him unless he accepted the commandments of God and the instructions of the community council. Vermes[110] shares similar views.

Genuine repentance and an adoption of a new way of life must accompany the lustration according to Sutcliffe.[111] Schubert[112] and McKenzie[113] express the same idea. Along with them, Dupont-Sommer,[114] Van Der Ploeg,[115] and LaSor[116] advance the same theory that some form of repentance on the part of the candidate is necessary when he enters the baths or washings. However, none of them believes that the water itself has the power to purify the candidate. Ringgren[117] implies that repentance is necessary but adds that it is a prerequisite for participation in the common meal. Scholars like Stauffer,[118] Smyth,[119] De Vaux,[120] Albright,[121] Benoit,[122] and Blau[123] state simply that the Qumranians practiced daily ritual baths of purification.

Harrison,[124] however, is explicit in his denial of the need for repentance before the candidate undergoes the ritual ablution. Finally, Murphy and Rowley make very cautious statements. The Qumranians practiced many sacred lustrations, but Murphy[125] does not specify what he means by sacred. At first, Rowley states that the Qumranian washings in the passage of the <u>Manual of Discipline</u> probably refer to the first ritual lustrations of the day.[126] Later, he adds that the ritual bathing act which is a total immersion is meaningless without the spirit to validate it.

It seems that, in light of Borwnlee's and Vermes' translations of passages from the <u>Manual of Discipline</u> (3:4-9; 5:13-14) that the scholars who support the theory that some form of repentance on the part of the neophyte must accompany the ritual washings have the stronger case.

19

2. The Qumran Ablutions or Lustrations Were Baptismal Rites

There are scholars who believe that the Qumran washings were more than ablutions or lustrations, with or without the need for repentance. They claim that these washings were baptismal rites. Cross[127] and Steinmann[128] say that the washings were definitely a baptism but they are not sure as to all the conditions and frequency of the washings. According to Robinson,[129] the Qumran washings were a baptism in the sense that they repudiated the past and they emphasized repentance. It could be received repeatedly. It was a baptism, Cullman[130] says, because it admitted the candidate into the fellowship of the community. Black[131] makes a further clarification, saying that it was a baptism of repentance for the remission of sins, but not in the full sense of Christian baptism which has no purification significance. For Leaney,[132] it was a baptism of water and spirit.

Wright[133] states that the initiatory rite was a baptismal rite, which was repeated at intervals as a sign of purification from evil thoughts and intentions. It is called a baptism with double significance, a ritual purity and an act of atonement. Gordon[134] infers that baptism took place when he states that baptismal pools were found at Qumran. Finally, John Heron summarizes his position by saying that the initiatory rite was initiation by baptism with immersion in running water accompanied by the recitation of the Decalogue and confession of sin followed by participation in a sacred meal of bread and wine.[135]

Neither Brownlee's nor Vermes' translations of the Manual of Discipline (3:4-9; 5:13-14; 6:14-23) support the theory that it was a baptism of water and spirit. Their translations (3:4-5; 6:8-9) substantiate the theories of scholars who maintain that the Qumran baptism was meaningless unless it was associated with repentance. However, Heron's theory finds support in Vermes' translation (MD 6:16-17), but not in Brownlee's. Vermes' translation states that the neophyte could not participate in the Pure Meal until one year was completed.

3. The Qumran Ablutions of Lustrations Were Rites with or without a Baptismal Ceremony

There are scholars who believe that the Qumran ablutions refer to a rite of initiation accompanied by a lustration or a baptismal ceremony. It is the opinion of Driver[136] that it was

a rite of initiation accompanied by a lustration with the prerequisite of repentance. Finegan,[137] Milik,[138] Brown,[139] and
Brownlee[140] agree with Driver. In addition to the lustration
and the need of repentance, Pryke[141] says that the rite of
initiation included a solemn oath to obey the rules of the
community. Allegro[142] proposes that the Qumranians practiced a
rite of initiation probably followed by a baptism ceremony. It
appears that the theories of Finegan, Milik, Brown, Driver, and
Pryke may be supported by both Brownlee's and Vermes' translations (MD 3:6, 8-9, 6:14-23).

4. The Qumran Ablutions or Lustrations Were Sacramental Rites

There are few scholars who claim that these washings or
baths were sacramental. Beasley-Murray[143] contends that the
Qumran lustrations had some sacramental efficacy. Perhaps
Millar Burrows gives the clearest expression of this position
when he says, "These baths were sacramental but the 'mediation'
was no more and no less sacramental than it was in the atonement
rites of the Old Testament."[144] Neither Brownlee's nor Vermes'
translation indicates whether words were used at the Qumran
moral washings. Brownlee gives a clue that these moral washings
were self administered, which is evident from passages in the
Manual of Discipline. (3:4-5, 9) However, Vermes' translation is
not clear on this point. It may be interpreted that these moral
washings were self administered or administered by another.

5. The Word "Touch," in the Translations of the Manual of
   Discipline

In addition to the problem of identifying whether the
Qumranians practiced ritual and moral ablutions, lustrations, or
baptisms, scholars differ on the interpretation of certain words
and phrases in the passages in the Manual of Discipline. For
example, Driver[145] says that the word, "touch," in the two phrases
"not touch the Purity of the Many" and "not touch the Drink of
Many," refers to the common meal and not the washings at Qumran.
He states further that the word "touch" (Hebrew-Naga) does not
mean to eat or drink. He believes the word, "touch," refers to
the preparation of food and drink. Therefore, he concludes that
the candidates were not allowed to prepare the food and drink of
the full-fledged members of the community.

The translations (6:16-17; 20-21) of Brownlee and Vermes use the word, "touch" in conjunction with the phrases "Purity of the Many," "Drink of the Many," "the Pure Meal of the Congregation," and "the Drink of the Congregation." From their silence on the interpretation of the word, "touch," it may be assumed that it is to be understood as touch in the English sense of the word.[146]

6. The Word, "Many," in the Translations of the Manual of Discipline

Authorities like Burrows claim that the Hebrew word usually translated as "many" is the ordinary meaning in Hebrew. But in Aramaic the same word means "much" or "great ones." Therefore, Burrows concludes that the full-fledged lay members of the community were "the Many" to the priestly leaders and, to the candidates in training, the priests were the "Great Ones." There is evidence at Qumran that Hebrew and Aramaic were the languages of the community. However, LaSor[147] says that the word, "many," may mean "the Many" (in number), or it may mean "the Great Ones," "the Chiefs." He concludes that it may mean: 1) the entire community, 2) the majority in any given action, or 3) a ruling body in the community.

Delorme[148] and McKenzie[149] interpret "many" to mean the full-fledged members of the community who could only be admitted to meals after the baths. For Schubert,[150] "many" means men of holiness and for Leaney[151] it signifies men of the Holy One, that is God. Obviously, there is lack of agreement among scholars on this point.

Although Brownlee[152] interprets the term "the Many" as a technical term for membership, Vermes is silent on this point. Vermes does not use the term "the Many" in his translation but rather the terms "Saints" (5:13-14) and "Congregation." (6:16-17, 20-21)

7. The Phrase "Purity of the Many" in the Translations of the Manual of Discipline

Just as the word "many" has a variety of interpretations among scholars, so too does the phrase "Purity of the Many." Vermes[153] interprets it to mean the daily meals prepared according to ritual purity. According to Pryke,[154] and Baron and Blau,[155] it means common food or the common meal. LaSor[156] simply says that it means sacred food. As indicated in his works, Rowley[157] believes it refers to their daily ablutions. Sutcliffe[158] says it refers to the full-fledged members of the community.

In Vermes' translation of the Manual of Discipline (6:16-17) one reads "He shall not touch the Pure Meal of the Congregation." As has been stated, Vermes interprets the "Purity of the Many" to mean daily meals prepared according to ritual purity. However, Brownlee's translation (MD 6:16-17) reads, "He must not touch the Purity of the Many." According to him, it could refer to the lustrations at Qumran or it could have a wider meaning, including such items as sectarian food, or even the bodies of holy men in full membership.[159] Obviously, the exact meaning of the phrase "Purity of the Many" cannot be determined from the available works of scholars.

8. The Phrase, "Drink of the Many" in the Translations of the Manual of Discipline

Scholars also are divided on their interpretation of the phrase, "Drink of the Many." In general, they believe it refers either to food or drink. Milik[160] says that it refers to their sacred meals. This opinion also is shared by Rowley.[161] On the other hand, Sutcliffe[162] and Leaney[163] state that it refers to the preparation of the drink (liquids) at their meals. LaSor[164] calls it a sacred drink. The candidate for admission was neither allowed to prepare the liquids nor drink them at the common meal of the full-fledged members of the community. Pryke[165] concludes that the phrase means the liquids, especially wine, consumed at the common meal.

Brownlee's translation (MD 6:20) says, "He shall not touch the drink of the Many." In his translation, he does not say what he thinks this phrase means. He simply indicates what other scholars think it means.[166] Brownlee says Burrows suggests that this phrase may be used for the whole meal instead of the drink alone. Furthermore, he says that Sukenik is of the opinion that the phrase, "Drink of the Many" may mean to withhold the drink of knowledge from the thirsty. Vermes,[167] in his translation (MD 6:20), states, "He shall not touch the drink of the congregation." He understands the phrase, "Drink of the Many," to mean daily meals prepared in accordance with special ritual purity. I think it is a reasonable assumption that the precise identification of this phrase is not yet possible.

Briefly, then, it is apparent that scholars in their varying interpretations of the Manual of Discipline scroll are not universally in agreement. In fact, at times, some are completely opposed to one another. However, it must be remembered that Brownlee's and Vermes' translation of the Manual of Discipline have given a clearer picture of the meaning of certain words and phrases in this scroll. These men have helped to narrow down the wide spectrum of possible solutions. Their translations and interpretations provide a standard against which the interpretations of other scholars can be evaluated.

SUMMARY

From the collected data, several theories have been proposed concerning the identity of the group responsible for the settlement at Qumran. They have been identified as Pharisees, Sadducees, Zealots and Essenes. Although the evidence favors the Essene theory, it is not a proven fact. It seems to me that there is a real danger in making the assumption that these people were Essenes or members of some form of the Essene movement. This may prejudice the reader, consciously or unconsciously. Therefore, I prefer to use the term, Qumranians, since there is presently no other identification in the translated literature of Qumran.

The Qumran site is in Palestine approximately ten miles south of Jericho,[168] or sixteen miles east of Jerusalem.[169] Its second occupation (4 B.C. - 68 A.D.) is accepted by many scholars such as Burrows,[170] LaSor,[171] and Cross.[172]

As far as the date of the scrolls is concerned, a few scholars, among whom the best known is Solomon Zeitlin,[173] maintain that the scrolls are medieval forgeries. Many scholars like LaSor[174] are of the opinion that the scrolls were produced during the last century and a half B.C. and the first half of the first century A.D.

The discovery of the scrolls provides evidence that there were sectarian Jewish movements that challenged certain practices in

Judaism in the first century A.D. Although Qumran was one of these sectarian movements at this time, it is clear from their religious beliefs that they were basically Jewish and not Christian, as some scholars have maintained. In fact, they shared many of the current Jewish eschatological and Messianic expectations of their era, with the exception that they believed they were the "elect remnant" who would do penance for themselves and their nation and usher in the "New Era of the Messiah."

The Qumranians were Jews who voluntarily separated from their contemporaries in Palestine to live an austere and ascetic life. Among their religious practices were ablutions and lustrations, or what some scholars call "baptisms" or moral washings. Furthermore, archaeologists have discovered cisterns and basins that were used at Qumran but apparently the purpose for which they were used cannot be identified specifically. Neither do the translated texts give a clue as to their purposes. The Qumranians did practice ritual washings, which in themselves did not cleanse man from his sins, but whether these washings were some form of a "baptism" is certainly not clear from the translated texts. When scholars use the word, baptism, it would be well to know exactly in what sense they are using the word, that is, in the Jewish sense of the word or the Christian. Although the translated texts do not identify the type of washings that took place at Qumran, neither do the writings of scholars.

There is no consensus among scholars in their identification of the Qumranian washings. Since the word baptism is ambiguous and the translated passages of the texts are scanty, it would be more accurate to say that moral ritual washings took place at Qumran.

At this point, I believe that it is too soon to settle the above problems. When the remainder of the Qumran literature is translated, then perhaps a clearer picture of the language of the sect (terms such as "many," "purity,") and of the religious practices at Qumran will emerge.

Finally, the data suggests that the members of the Qumran community had a strong conviction that they were living in the last days. Therefore, they prepared for the final days by a strict observance of ritual and moral commands in the Torah (the Law).

CHAPTER 3

JOHN THE BAPTIST'S BAPTISM

The main source of material concerning John the Baptist is
the New Testament. In the New Testament, the fullest accounts
are found in Matthew, Mark and Luke. The material is not extensive, but one is able to sketch the life and ministry of John
from it. Of all the people who are mentioned in the New
Testament, none seems likely to have had a closer connection with
the Qumran community than John the Baptist. Millar Burrows said,
"There is no reason why one should be so reluctant to believe
that John was or had been a member of their community. The only
question is whether there is good reason to suppose that he was,
or that he had anything to do with the sect.[175]

IDENTIFICATION OF THE SYNOPTIC GOSPELS

The word gospel is a translation of the Greek, _evangelion_,
meaning the transmission of good news, but in the New Testament
it especially means the good news of salvation as preached by
Jesus of Nazareth in Palestine in the first century A.D.[176]
There are four gospels in the New Testament literature: Matthew,
Mark, Luke, and John.[177] The Synoptic Gospels are those written
by Matthew, Mark and Luke who lived in the first century A.D.[178]
If the contents of these three gospels compared, certain
literary relationships would be apparent[179] Therefore, they
have been commonly referred to as the Synoptic Gospels.

The similarity of material and notable dissimilarities within their writings, have given rise to the expression "the
synoptic problem."[180] Although there is agreement as to content,
arrangement, and language among the three writers, there are
differences as well. Briefly, the situation may be summarized as
follows: There are agreements and disagreements among the three
gospels; there are agreements and disagreements, particularly in
the writings of Matthew and Luke; there are sections that are
peculiar to one or the other of the three.

26

It is generally agreed among scholars that the synoptic gospels were written between 50 A.D. and 100 A.D. It is difficult to reconstruct the history that lies behind the written Synoptic Gospels. It can be done only with a small measure of certainty, and a portion of conjecture. It seems fairly certain that the Synoptic Gospels existed first in oral form, and it is likely that the oral form soon took on a definitive pattern or plan, or, perhaps, several patterns according to the region where it was preached. For example, Matthew's gospel was probably intended for the Jews of Palestine. It seems that he, like Mark and Luke, drew on the oral traditions in their accounts about the life of Jesus. Behind the written gospels, there were Christian communities in which the stories of Jesus were still circulating orally. It seems reasonable to assume that these communities found it necessary to write down the stories of Jesus' life including John the Baptist's Baptism. Those stories were repeated over and over. The studies of the ancient writers show something of what happens when a story is transmitted orally in a community. To keep a story interesting, ancient writers change indirect speech to direct, even though they do not know the exact words originally spoken. Questions are inserted to make sure the point of the story is not missed. A particular episode is sometimes repeated with different details. When, finally, the Synoptic Gospels were written down, there was all this material to draw on. The synoptics were not reporters who had taken down John the Baptist's activities, nor were they all eyewitnesses of the events they recorded. They probably drew on written documents and oral accounts in circulation in the communities they knew. Probably they utilized the material they inherited without checking each detail. Finally, each synoptic most likely had his own insight into the message of John, was impressed by different aspects of John's activities and was aware of the audience he had to address himself to.

Therefore, John's baptismal ministry was recorded in the synoptic gospels.

INTERPRETATION OF TERMS--RITE, SACRAMENT, AND BAPTISMS

Before examining the comparison of the Revised Standard Version and the Jerusalem Bible Version of the Synoptic Gospels of John the Baptist's baptism, it will be helpful to examine the meaning of terms such as rite, sacrament, and baptism.

Scholars use the terms rite, sacrament, and baptism to describe the baptism that John the Baptist performed. Briefly, the meaning of these words will be examined.

A rite, in general, is an external sign or action used in religious services, and designed either to express or to incite a corresponding internal religious feeling, as for example, the outstretching of hands in prayer.[181] At times, it may include all the ceremonies such as bows, anointings, immersions, connected with a particular religious practice or observance.[182] Sutcliffe[183] defines a rite as the external symbol of a spiritual action that does not produce the effect by itself. Since rite is a modern term, I have avoided the use of the term for the Qumranian baptisms and John the Baptist's baptism. I prefer to call them practices. A practice is less formal than a rite.

According to some scholars, a sacrament means an initiation into a particular group or association.[184] In addition, it is an external visible sign that produces interiorly, by the power of God, that same reality it signifies.[185] For example, in the rite of Christian baptism, the external washing produces an interior washing of the person's sins, despite the moral disposition of the person who is baptizing.[186] In other words, Harrison[187] says that a sacrament, as in Christian baptism, produces of itself a spiritual purity and moral rectitude. For the Christian, the effect of a sacrament comes from the redeeming death of Jesus who is the sole source of grace and salvation.[188] The church is the minister of these sacramental rites through her ministers.

Now the term, baptism, derived from the Greek noun baptisma means an immersion or washing with water, while the term to baptize, derived from the Greek verb, baptizo, means to dip or to dye.[189] To immerse for a religious purpose may be traced back to the book of Leviticus 14:8-9.[190] Boyer[191] says that the baptism means to immerse, and it designates the sacrament of Christian initiation. According to Conzelmann,[192] Cross,[193] and Landman, baptism means the universal rite of acceptance into the Christian community in the name of Jesus. For some scholars, the Greek word, baptizo, primarily means to dye and is usually associated with water as a rite of initiation into the Christian church.[194] Leon-DuFour,[195] however, says that the Greek verb, to baptize, primarily means to immerse, to wash, and therefore signifies an immersion or a washing. In summary, then, it must be remembered that the term baptism can be understood in a Jewish sense as well as a Christian sense. In the Jewish sense, it means a religious ablution, signifying purification or consecration.[196] In the

Christian sense, it means an initiatory rite into the Christian church by means of water and in the name of Jesus. Sacramental theology scarcely appears in the Synoptic Gospels at all. There is no single word that renders the idea, nor are there any passages that group those rites the church regards as sacraments under a common heading.

COMPARISON OF THE REVISED STANDARD VERSION AND THE JERUSALEM BIBLE VERSION OF THE SYNOPTIC GOSPELS

In this section, I will examine the Revised Standard Version and the Jerusalem Bible Version of the Synoptic Gospels for similarities and differences concerning the baptism rite of John the Baptist. In the analysis, the following categories emerged:

Wilderness

The R.S.V. and J.B.V. translations of the gospels reveal that John the Baptist received a call from God in the wilderness of Judea. Also, they indicate that he preached in the same area. All three gospel accounts are unanimous about John the Baptist's ministry taking place in the wilderness of Judea. The two translations of this passage are virtually the same.

	Revised Standard Version	Jerusalem Bible Version
Matthew 3:1-2	In those days came John the Baptist, preaching in the wilderness of Judea.	In due course John the Baptist appeared; he preached in the wilderness of Judaea.
Mark 1:4	John the baptizer appeared in the wilderness.	John the Baptist appeared in the wilderness.
Luke 3:2	The word of God came to John the son of Zechariah in the wilderness	The word of God came to John, the son of Zechariah in the wilderness.

A Priest's Son

Only Luke's gospel records that John was the son of Zechariah. In chapter one of Luke's gospel, one reads that Zechariah belonged to the Abijah section of the priesthood and he had a wife, Elizabeth, by name. In her old age, she conceived and gave birth to a son and they called him John, as the angel of God

29

had instructed Zechariah. Therefore, John was the son of a priest.

	Revised Standard Version	Jerusalem Bible Version
Luke 3:2	The word of God came to John the son of Zechariah.	The word of God came to John son of Zechariah in the wilderness.

The Message

Although the R.S.V. and J.B.V. translations (Matthew 3:2-3; Mark 1:4-5; Luke 3:3-4) are substantially the same, there are slight variances. For example, R.S.V. (Mark 1:4-5) reads "preaching a baptism" and the J.B.V. (Mark 1:4-5) reads, "Proclaiming a baptism." However, all three synoptics write the same points about John's ministry: 1) He preached a message of repentance. 2) His baptism was a baptism of repentance needed for the forgiveness of sins. 3) He preached in the region around the Jordan. 4) The "Last Days" were at hand.

	Revised Standard Version	Jerusalem Bible Version
Matthew 3:2-3	Repent, for the kingdom of heaven² is at hand.	Repent, for the kingdom of heaven is close at hand.
Mark 1:4-5	Preaching a baptism of repentance for the forgiveness of sins.	Proclaiming a baptism of repentance for the forgiveness of sins.
Luke 3:3-4	He went into all the region about the Jordan, preaching a baptism of repentance for the forgiveness of sins.	He went through the whole Jordan district proclaiming a baptism of repentance for the forgiveness of sins.

Isaiah's Prophecy

The three synoptic writers all quote the introductory words of the Old Testament passage (Isaiah 40:3), "The Voice cries: In the wilderness prepare the way of the Lord make strait in the desert a highway for our God." The emphasis seems to be on the voice crying in the wilderness, because John used his voice to call people to repentance. None of the synoptic writers placed these words on John's own lips.

	Revised Standard Version	Jerusalem Bible Version
Matthew 3:3	The Voice of one crying in the wilderness: prepare the way of the Lord, make his paths straight.	A voice cries in the wilderness: prepare a way for the Lord, make his paths straight.
Mark 1:2	Behold, I send my messenger before thy face, who shall prepare the way: the voice of one crying in the wilderness: Prepare the way of the Lord, make his paths straight.	Look, I am going to send my messenger before you: he will prepare your way. A voice cries in the wilderness: prepare a way for the Lord, make his paths straight.
Luke 3:4-6	The voice of one crying in the wilderness: prepare the way of the Lord, make his paths straight. Every valley shall be filled and every mountain and hill be brought low, and the crooked shall be made straight, and the rough ways shall be made smooth; and all flesh shall see the salvation of God.	A voice cries in the wilderness prepare a way for the Lord, make his paths straight. Every valley will be filled in, every mountain and hill be laid low, winding ways will be straightened and rough roads made smooth. And all mankind shall see the salvation of God.

Baptism (the Minister, the Receiver and Place of Baptism)

All of the synoptic writers record the minister, the receiver and place of John's baptism. However, they vary on details. For example, Luke (3:12) notes that tax collectors were among those who came to be baptized. Matthew's and Mark's accounts do not mention them.

The comparison of the R.S.V. and the J.B.V. translations reveals that they are quite similar. The difference is in the arrangement of words rather than in the substitution of words. Neither translation adds or subtracts anything from the other. The comparison of the translations indicates the following points: 1) John baptized, 2) John baptized in the river Jordan, 3) those

being baptized confessed their sins either before, during or after
their baptism, 4) the recipients of John's baptism came from
Jerusalem, all of Judea and the whole Jordan district, 5) the
recipients of John's baptism were tax collectors, Pharisees and
Sadducees, probably soldiers and others who are not identified
specifically, 6) apparently Jews were the receipients of John's
baptism but there is no indication that non-Jews were excluded
from it, 7) there is no indication that men alone were baptized,
8) John baptized with water, 9) the manner of baptizing is not
clear from the translations, probably it was some form of
immersion.

	Revised Standard Version	Jerusalem Bible Version
Matthew 3:5-7	Then went out to him Jerusalem and all Judea and the region about the Jordan, and they were baptized by him in the river of Jordan confessing their sins. But when he saw many of the Pharisees and Sadducees coming for baptism.	Then Jerusalem and all Judaea and the whole Jordan district made their way to him, and they were baptised by him in the river Jordan they confessed their sins. But when he saw a number of Pharisees and Sadducees coming for baptism.
Mark 1:5-6	And there went out to him all the country of Judea and all the people of Jerusalem; and they were baptized by him in the river Jordan, confessing their sins.	All Judaea and all the people of Jerusalem made their way to him and as they were baptised by him in the river Jordan they confessed their sins.
Luke 3:12	Tax collectors also came to be baptized.	There were tax collectors too who came for baptism.
Luke 3:14	Soldiers also asked him, and we, what shall we do?	Some soldiers asked him in their turn, what about us?

John's Baptism Was a Preparation for Another Baptism

From the Synoptic Gospels (Matthew 3:13, 16; Mark 1:9,10;

Luke 3:21), it seems that John's baptism was temporary and preparatory for a future baptism. The latter baptism would be performed
by someone greater than John. John prophesied a future baptism
with holy spirit and fire by the Coming One. Matthew's and
Luke's gospels record that the future baptism would be a baptism
of the Holy Spirit and Fire, whereas Mark's gospel says that
it would be a baptism of the Holy Spirit. Thus, it is not
clear whether John is proclaiming two baptisms or one.

	Revised Standard Version	Jerusalem Bible Version
Matthew 3:11	I baptize you with water for repentance but he who is coming after me is mightier than I, whose sandals I am not worthy to carry; he will baptize you with the Holy Spirit and with Fire.	I baptise you in water for repentance, but the one who follows me is more powerful than I am, and I am not fit to carry his sandals; he will baptise you with the Holy Spirit and Fire.
Mark 1:8	I have baptized you with water; but he will baptize you with the Holy Spirit.	I have baptised you with water, but he will baptise you with the Holy Spirit.
Luke 3:16-17	I baptize you with water; but he who is mightier than I is coming, the thong of whose sandals I am not worthy to untie; he will baptize you with the Holy Spirit and with Fire	I baptise you with water, but someone is coming, someone who is more powerful than I am and I am not fit to undo the strap of his sandals; he will baptise you with the Holy Spirit and Fire.

BIBLICAL SCHOLAR'S OPINIONS

How have scholars interpreted these synoptic passages? For
purposes of clarity, I have grouped my findings under seven
headings.

1. John's Baptism Was Not a Baptism of Initiation

Sutcliffe[197] says there is no evidence that John wished to found a religious brotherhood but rather to efface himself and to promote the interest of the founder of the kingdom. I believe that Sutcliffe's position is reasonable, since John's baptism seemed to be temporary. His baptism is preparatory for the permanent one to come. Luke's gospel (3:16-17) states, "I baptize you with water; but he who is mightier than I is coming, the thong of whose sandals I am not worthy to untie; he will baptize you with the Holy Spirit and with Fire."

2. John's Baptism Was an Eschatological Baptismal Sacrament

There are scholars who hold the opinion that John's Baptism was an eschatological baptismal sacrament. As Bultmann[198] explains, "It meant the person would be purified for the coming kingdom of God and would belong to the company of those who would escape wrath and judgement of God." Stauffer[199] says that John's act of baptism was bound up with the historical figure, Jesus, who would baptize with the spirit of God rather than just water. Finally, Robinson[200] believes that John's baptism forced the appearance of Jesus and his baptism of salvation.

John's mission was eschatological in that he was preparing the way for the Messiah. For him, Jesus was the Messiah. Therefore, it can be assumed that John's baptism was eschatological. In Matthew's gospel (3:2-3), it is stated, "Repent for the kingdom of heaven is at hand."

3. John's Baptism is a Unique Baptism

Some scholars are cautious in identifying the type of baptism John performed. For example, Steinmann[201] says that his baptism brought a new birth. It prepared the whole man for an encounter with the coming judge, says Schlink.[202] For Conzelmann[203] John's baptism was the opening of a new life and the end of the past life of a person. His baptism was a connection with and not a contrast to the one who would come after him.[204] Goppelt[205] calls John's baptism an initial cleansing that mediates the blotting out of sins.

John's baptism was unique in the sense that it was an immediate preparation for the permanent baptism to come, which would be better than his and any other. Luke's gospel (3:16-17) records, "I baptize you with water but he who is mightier than I is coming, the thong of whose sandals I am not worthy to untie; he will baptize you with the Holy Spirit and with Fire." John's baptism

34

was also unique because it was open to all types of people, and there was no period of probation. Mark's gospel (1:5-6) says that they went out to him from Jerusalem, and different parts of Judea to be baptized. Luke's gospel (3:12-14) records that tax collectors and soldiers came to him to be baptized.

4. John's Baptism is a Preparation for the Baptism of Spirit to Come

There are scholars who see John's baptism as a preparation for the future of the Spirit. Delorme[206] sees John's baptism as a preparation for the baptism of the Spirit and Fire rather than as two distinctive baptisms, a baptism of Spirit and a baptism of Fire. However, Scobie[207] believes that his baptism was in preparation for two distinctive baptisms to come, namely, a baptism of Spirit for the good people and a baptism of Fire for the wicked. According to Brownlee,[208] John's baptism was probably a preparation for one future baptism, that of the Spirit and Fire. Those who accepted John's baptism would receive the baptism of Spirit, and those who refused or underwent it hypo-critically would be punished by Fire.[209] John may have been alluding to the Qumranian hymn, which depicts an eschatological river of Fire, when he speaks of a baptism of Fire.[210] For Torrance,[211] the fire idea denotes a radical judgment of the spirit that would take place imminently after John's baptism. Finally, some scholars say that John's baptism was a preparation for another baptism, which would bring a universal and definitive judgment.[212] These scholars find support from the Synoptic Gospel accounts. Matthew (3:11), Mark (1:8), and Luke (3:16-17) record that John said he was baptizing with water but one greater than he will come and baptize with the Holy Spirit and Fire. Therefore, I certainly share these scholars' point of view.

5. John's Baptism Was Like the Jewish Proselyte Baptisms with the Rite of Initiation, Immersion and Repentance

For some scholars, John's baptism was modeled on an adapta-tion of the Jewish proselyte baptisms. For example, scholars such as Leon-DuFour,[213] Moore, Allen, and Buttrick,[214] believe that John's baptism was an extension, innovation, or an adaptation of the Jewish proselyte baptisms. Whitely[215] agrees with these scholars but adds that John's baptism stressed morality. Ac-cording to Rowley,[216] John's baptism was more like the Jewish proselyte baptisms than the Qumranians. However, John's baptism was different in some ways. It was public and universal to Jew and non-Jew[217] Gilmore[218] believes that John's baptisms were more like the Qumranian baptisms than the Jewish proselyte baptisms.

From the evidence at hand, it seems to me that it is impossible to determine whether or not John modeled, adapted, or innovated his baptism on the Jewish proselyte baptism, since it is impossible to establish that the latter was in existence prior to John's ministry. Even if one assumes Jewish proselyte baptisms were in existence, it is almost impossible to determine how widespread they were or if John himself knew about them.

6. John's Baptism Was a Baptism of Water With the Need of Repentance for the Remission of Sins

Fritsch,[219] Allegro,[220] Ringgren,[221] Boyer,[222] Leon-DuFour,[223] and Roth and Wigoder[224] say that John's baptism was a water-baptism which demanded repentance for the remission of sins. However, they do not say whether it was administered to both Jew and non-Jew. Both Black[225] and Guillet[226] add that John's baptism was for all. Finally, Beasley-Murray[227] and Dunn[228] believe that John the Baptist was influenced by the Qumranian baptisms. On the other hand, Murphy[229] does not completely share their opinion. He says that the possibility exists that both John and the Qumran community were reflections of a widespread Baptist movement during this period.[230] Therefore, it may be assumed that John's ideas were not influenced solely by the Qumran Community. In fact, Murphy mentions that the Qumranians encouraged many sacred lustrations, which were repeated frequently, unlike John's baptism, which was not repeated.[231]

It seems reasonable to assume that John would have been influenced by a baptismal sect like the Qumranian community since he preached and baptized in the same general vicinity of Qumran. It is highly unlikely that he would not have been aware of their baptismal practices.

7. John's Baptism Was a Water-Baptism, a Rite of Initiation, Administered Only Once, and Was Offered to Jews and Non-Jews

There are scholars such as Harrison,[232] Cullmann,[233] Conzelmann,[234] Driver,[235] Benoit,[236] LaSor,[237] and Kittel and

Bromley,[238] who believe that John's baptism was a water-baptism, a rite of initiation, administered but once to Jews and non-Jews alike.

Brownlee[239] shares the opinion of these scholars but adds that John's baptism was in public. In his article, Delorme[240] adds that there was no probationary period for those receiving John's baptism. Although Danielou,[241] Robinson,[242] Schubert,[243] and Brown[244] also express the same opinion as the former scholars, yet they believe that John probably received his orientation from Qumran.

While scholars vary in their interpretation of John the Baptist's baptism, they give us new insights into this complete problem.

SUMMARY

In summary, then, the Synoptic Gospels are those written by Matthew, Mark, and Luke who lived in the first century A.D. These writings discuss John the Baptist's ministry, especially his baptismal practice. Although the vocabulary, figures of speech, and content are similar in the synoptics, there are differences. For instance, in Matthew's account (3:11), he says that John's baptism is a preparation for a future baptism, a baptism of Spirit and Fire. However, Mark (1:8) says that it will be a baptism of Spirit. Various attempts have been made to reconcile the differences in the synoptic writings, but there has been little success.

The Synoptic Gospels were written between 50-100 A.D. If the theory that the Qumranian writings were completed by 70 A.D. is true, then both literatures were contemporary.

The Synoptic Gospels speak of John the Baptist's ministry taking place in or near the Jordan river at a location or locations that cannot be positively identified. Besides, it seems that John was born in a village about twenty miles from Qumran. John's appearance and message give the impression of an ascetic. The synoptic accounts say that John received his call while he was in the "wilderness." The general meaning of "wilderness" is the desert of Judea in Palestine. It seems, then, from the data collected that John the Baptist preached and baptized in the general vicinity of Qumran. Scholars suggest a possible connection between John and Qumran. A few scholars say that John the Baptist was a member of the Qumran community. More scholars favor the view that he was in contact with Qumran and, therefore, was influenced by their religious practices, especially their baptisms. This latter view seems more probable to the researcher. However, there are scholars who believe that John the Baptist was influenced by the Jewish proselyte baptisms of the first century A.D. in Palestine. It is not a positive fact that Jewish proselyte baptisms were practiced in Palestine prior to John's ministry. Therefore, John the Baptist seems to have been influenced more by the baptismal practices of Qumran than by Jewish proselyte baptisms.

The difference between John's baptisms and the Qumranian baptisms seems to be in John's preparation for a future baptism that would take place. He says it will be administered by one greater than he, and he alludes to its being a more effective type of baptism. John seems to offer his own baptism to Jew and non-Jew. His baptism does not appear to be self-administered. It was probably administered by him. It is impossible to determine whether the form used was total immersion, partial immersion, or immersion at all. He does attach the condition of repentance to his baptism. Whether or not a confession of sins was demanded before, during, or after the baptism is not certain. Finally, John seems to administer it publicly, not privately. It has been questioned whether it was a rite of initiation, in the sense that John was forming a new community. Once again, it is impossible to give positive answers to the question.

On the other hand, the Qumranian "baptisms" were apparently not in preparation for a future "baptism." Only Jews were baptized and the Qumran "baptisms" seem to have been self-administered. The rites may have been initiatory for the new candidates being admitted into the Qumran community but more likely they were ritual moral washings. Like John the Baptist, the Qumranians demanded repentance from their followers. Unlike John's baptism, the Qumranian "baptisms" were apparently private.

In summary, then, John's baptism was apparently a water-baptism in preparation for a baptism of Spirit and Fire to be administered by someone greater than he. Probably it was administered to Jews and non-Jews by John himself. Finally, some Christian scholars prefer to call John's baptism a sacramental or a sacrament. These terms are primarily later Christian interpretations. Perhaps they give a meaning to John's baptism that was not intended by him. It would be better not to apply these terms to his baptism and let the facts speak for themselves.

In conclusion, I agree with Burrows who says, "John and the covenanters (Qumranians) represent two movements which are in some respects parallel, but in the main lines independent of each other."[245]

CHAPTER 4

COMPARISONS AND CONCLUSIONS

From the material discussed some comparisons and conclusions are possible:

COMPARISONS

For this comparative analysis I have examined the collected data under three categories: words, elements, and actions.

1. Words

Formula "I will baptize you with water"

The Manual of Discipline (3:4-9; 5:13-14; 6:14-23 B.V.; V.V.) gives no indication that the Qumranians used a particular formula in their baptismal rites when a neophyte was admitted or a lapsed member was reinstated into the community.

Likewise, the Synoptic Gospels (Matthew 3:11; Mark 1:8; Luke 3:16-17) do not record a formula that John the Baptist may have used when he baptized in the Jordan river. Although no specific formula is recorded, these passages seem to indicate the possibility that a formula may have been used by John. Matthew (3:11) reads, "I baptize you with water" and "I baptize you in water." Mark (1:8) says, "I have baptized you with water." Luke (3:16-17) notes that John said, "I baptize you with water." Matthew's (3:11) and Luke's (3:16-17) accounts say John foretold that another would come after him, and he would baptize with the Holy Spirit and with Fire. In Mark's (1:8) account, there is no mention of the phrase "with fire."

In conclusion, I believe that a formula may have been used by both the Qumranians and John the Baptist, but it was not recorded. It seems highly improbable that some type of formula would not have been used, since a formula is usually a sign of

identification with an act, an object, or a person. The
Qumranians may not have recorded a formula since they were a
secretive sect. Likewise, John the Baptist may have feared the
Jewish and Roman authorities. At the present time, there is no
record of a "baptismal" formula used by the Qumranians or John
the Baptist.

"Holy Spirit and/or Fire"

The use of words like "Holy Spirit and Fire" (Matthew 3:11;
Luke 3:16-17) has caused several scholars to see a parallel with
the Manual of Discipline (3:6-9).

The Manual of Discipline (3:6-7) states, "For it is through
the spirit of God's true counsel" (B.V.)and "For it is through
the spirit of true counsel." (V.V.) In another passage of the
Manual of Discipline (3:8-9), one reads, "through an upright and
humble spirit that his sins will be atoned" (B.V.) and "He shall
be cleansed from all sins by the spirit of holiness uniting him
to his truth."

In the synoptic accounts (Matthew 3:11; Mark 1:8; Luke
3:16-17), the words "Holy Spirit" are mentioned. Neither Matthew,
Mark, nor Luke says that John baptized with the Holy Spirit and/or
Fire, but that he was to be followed by one who would. Matthew
(3:11) states, "I baptize you with water for repentance but he
who is coming after me is mightier than I, whose sandals I am not
worthy to carry; he will baptize you with the Holy Spirit and with
Fire." Mark's account (1:8) records, "I have baptized you with
water; but he will baptize you with the Holy Spirit." Luke's
Gospel (3:16-17) says, "I baptize you with water; but he who is
mightier than I is coming, the thong of whose sandals I am not
worthy to untie; he will baptize you with the Holy Spirit and with
Fire."

The problem is whether the word "Spirit" means Holy Spirit,
or the spirit of man or God or has some other meaning. Is it
justifiable to say that John borrowed the word "Spirit" from the
Qumranians? From the evidence, I do not think so. Many Jews
would be familiar with the Book of Exekiel. (36:25-27) This book
refers to "Spirit." Since the book of Ezekiel is older than the
Manual of Discipline and the Synoptic writings, the word "Spirit"
was not exclusive with the Qumranians. Therefore, John's use of
the word does not necessarily stem from the Manual of Discipline.

Probably, he was using the words "Holy Spirit" in the same way the Qumranians and other Jews would have understood it, the spirit of God. There is no evidence that the Qumranians and John the Baptist understood "Spirit" or "Holy Spirit" in the sense of later Christian theology. Christians generally understand "Spirit" or "Holy Spirit" to mean the third person of God, the Holy Spirit.

2. Elements

The Manual of Discipline (3:9 B.V., V.V.) and the Synoptic Gospels (Matthew 3:11; Mark 1:8; Luke 3:16-17) indicate that water was used for baptisms. Brownlee's and Vermes' translations (MD 3:9) indicate that the Qumranians baptized with rippling water and cleansing water. Obviously there is a difference of opinion as to what the original text means; thus the issue remains unsettled. The use of running, rippling or still water is not clear from the Manual of Discipline (3:9). Likewise, the synoptic writers (Matthew 3:11; Mark 1:8; Luke 3:16-17) state that John baptized with water. For example, Mark's account (1:8) says, "I have baptized you with water." Consequently, a detailed comparison of the type of water used by either group is impossible.

3. Actions

Place

According to the translations used, the place where the Qumranians performed their "baptisms" is not mentioned in the Manual of Discipline. Based on archaeological evidence, apparently there were cisterns and basins in the settlement. Scholars are uncertain about the purpose of these cisterns and basins. They may or may not have been used for "baptismal" purposes. Since the Qumranians were within two or three miles of the Jordan river, it is possible that they may have used the river for baptisms. However, they probably did not use the river Jordan. It must be remembered that even a journey of one mile probably proved difficult for these people. Second, the Jordan river is not mentioned in the Manual of Discipline. Third, the streams of Ain Feshka were near to the Qumran settlement. Fourth, the Qumran community was very much concerned about contamination and, therefore, would probably have avoided the Jordan river. They most likely would have used their own cisterns or basins which would not have been defiled by the unclean.

The area of baptism poses a debatable question. Matthew

(3:5-7) and Mark (1:5-6) relate that John baptized in the Jordan river. Matthew (3:5-6) records, "Then went out to him Jerusalem and all Judea and the region about the Jordan, and they were baptized by him in the river Jordan confessing their sins." Mark (1:5-6) states, "And there went out to him all the country of Judea and all the people of Jerusalem; and they were baptized by him in the river Jordan, confessing their sins." It seems clear from these passages that John's baptismal ministry was in and around the Jordan river.

Therefore, it is quite probable that John used the Jordan river, and the Qumranians used their cisterns and basins, both of which had geographical proximity and may have become a point of contact for both groups.

Recipients

The Manual of Discipline (3:4-6 B.V.) states, "He can not purify himself by atonement, not cleanse with water for impurity, nor sanctify himself with seas or rivers, nor cleanse himself with any water for washing. Unclean! Unclean! shall he be as long as he rejects God's Laws." Thus, the unclean person whether he be a neophyte or a lapsed member of the community had to be purified. Because of the nature of the Qumran sect, which was strictly Jewish, it is probable that only Jews were baptized. The Qumranians believed that they were doing penance for their fellow Jews, and so it seems unlikely that non-Jews were admitted into this community. The question of whether both men and women were baptized is not answered in the Manual of Discipline. Most evidence from Jewish sources points to the probable conclusion that it was the men who were baptized. Evidence also shows that the majority of people in the Qumran community were men despite the fact that skeletons of some women were found in the Qumran cemetery. Of course, there may be other places where the women were buried which have not yet been discovered.

Uncertainty as to whether John baptized non-Jews as well as Jews prevails in the synoptic accounts. These writings are silent about women being baptized. Matthew (3:5-7) and Mark (1:5-6) record that people from Jerusalem, all of Judea and the area of the Jordan came to be baptized by John. Luke (3:14) says, "Tax collectors also came to be baptized." One may speculate that both men and women sought entry into the new community being formed by John. Since John undertook this step in preparation

43

for the coming of the new leader who would be greater than himself, it is plausible that men and women, Jew and non-Jew, had to be baptized by John. John's mission seems to have been broader than the Qumranians. The Qumranians limited themselves to Jews alone. The <u>Manual of Discipline</u> (6:14 B.V.) states, "And everyone from Israel who dedicates himself to join the Council of Community."

Admittance

Brownlee's and Vermes' translations of the <u>Manual of Discipline</u> (6:14-23) indicate that certain procedures were to be followed for the admittance of new members to the Qumran community. According to their translations, a neophyte was first to be examined by an Overseer (Brownlee) or a Guardian (Vermes) who would decide on the neophyte's fitness to enter the Qumran community. Then, after an unspecified period, his case was to be considered by the members of the sect at a general meeting. If the members of the sect approved, he entered a probationary period for two years. Not until the first of these two years had passed was he allowed to share some aspects of community life. After a further year's probation, the candidate was accepted as a full-fledged member. In other words, there were stages of admittance to the Qumran community.

This probationary condition, however, is lacking in the synoptic accounts of John's baptism. Apparently, John baptized the neophyte immediately. There is no indication in the synoptic accounts that John or anyone examined the neophyte for fitness. John seems to be less selective in his membership. Matthew (3:5-7) states, "Then went out to him Jerusalem and all Judea and the region about the Jordan, and they were baptized by him in the river Jordan confessing their sins." Mark's account (1:5-6) reads, "And there went out to him the country of Judea and all the people of Jerusalem; and they were baptized by him in the river Jordan, confessing their sins." Luke's account (3:12) says, "Tax collectors also came to be baptized." Although Luke's account is less indicative than Matthew's and Mark's accounts, it still supports the theory that John did not demand a probationary period prior to his baptism. This reinforces the belief that John's mission to baptize people was wider in scope than the Qumranians.

The Minister

The question of who it was that performed the act of
baptism is one that the Manual of Discipline does not answer
clearly. Scholars speculate that one of the fifteen leaders of
the council may have been the minister of the Qumranian
"baptisms." This might have been the function of a member who
was considered to be the chief leader of the Qumran community.
The Manual of Discipline (6:14-15 B.V.) states, "And if he
(neophyte) grasps instruction, he (Overseer) shall bring him into
the convenant to turn to the truth and to turn away from all
perversity." However, the Manual (3:9 B.V.) also says, "He may
purify himself with rippling water." Vermes translates the same
passage (3:9), "And when his flesh is sprinkled with purifying
water and sanctified by cleansing water." It seems that Brownlee's
and Vermes' translations (MD 3:9) differ. Brownlee implies that
the Qumranian "baptisms" were self-administered and Vermes'
indicates that it is another person who administers the baptisms
on the neophyte. At this point, it is an open question as to
who administered the Qumranian "baptisms."

Unlike the Manual of Discipline of the Qumranians, the Synoptic Gospels say that John baptized the neophyte. Matthew
(3:5-6) states, "Then went out to him Jerusalem and all Judea and
the region about the Jordan, and they were baptized by him in
the river Jordan." Mark (1:6 R.S.V.) notes, "And they were
baptized by him in the river Jordan." Luke's account (3:7)
says, "He said therefore to the multitudes that came out to be
baptized by him." It seems relatively certain that John baptized
the neophytes.

The Method of Administration

The method of administration is not clear from either the
Qumranian Manual of Discipline or the Synoptic Gospels. Brownlee's
translation of the Manual of Discipline (3:9) says, "So that he
may purify himself with water for impurity and sanctify himself
with rippling water." On the other hand, Vermes' translation
(MD 3:9) reads, "And when his flesh is sprinkled with purifying
water and sanctified by cleansing water." Brownlee's translation gives no indication as to the manner the Qumranian "baptisms"
were administered. If Vermes' translation is more accurate, then
it would seem that the Qumranian "baptisms" were done by

45

sprinkling. Again, if Vermes is correct, were the Qumranians speaking in a literal or figurative sense? It seems that the Qumranian "baptisms" followed the traditional Jewish method of immersion. Jewish tradition shows that there were two types of immersion: complete immersion of the whole body, or partial immersion. These immersions were usually performed in a stream, spring, river or a Mikveh (pool). In addition to immersion, Jews did use the sprinkling of water on solemn occasions. Scholars generally use the terms ablution, lustration and baptism to describe the Qumranian administration of "baptism." By ablution they mean the Jewish idea of immersion. Lustration means some form of bathing. Their reference to baptism means a religious ablution signifying purification or consecration. It is difficult to determine exactly what scholars mean by these terms. Cross uses the term "lustration" meaning a sprinkling of water or a bath. The same terms, as used by Sutcliffe, means bathing. Scholars such as Wright, Robinson and Steinmann use the term baptism. Do these men use this term "baptism" in the Jewish sense as stated above, or in the Christian sense meaning "to dip in" or "under" as an initiatory rite into a specific group or community? Since it is not always possible to know exactly in what sense some scholars are using these terms, it cannot be assumed that the Qumranians used a form of immersion, sprinkling, or bathing. There is no consensus among scholars as to the method of "baptism" at Qumran.

Therefore, it seems reasonable to assume that the Qumranians used some form of immersion, since it was in common use in normative Judaism during these times.

The Snyoptic Gospels (Matthew 3:16; Mark 1:10) are the only indication that John's baptisms may have been done by immersion. Both passages refer to the baptism of Jesus by John. Matthew (3:16) states, "And when Jesus was baptized he went up immediately from the water." Mark's account (1:10) reads, "And when he came up out of the water." Luke's account of Jesus' baptism is silent on the manner of John's baptism of Jesus. The evidence from the gospel accounts of Matthew and Mark seem stronger than that in the Qumranian Manual of Discipline. Matthew and Mark imply that Jesus' baptism was done by some form of immersion. If Jesus was baptized by immersion, did John baptize other people by the same method? There does not seem to be any reason to think otherwise.

Some scholars, among whom are Allen and Conzelmann, say that John baptized by immersion. Others, like Rowley, say that John's baptism was a total immersion. Stauffer says it was an immersion up to the neck.

Scholars like Schlink are not sure what type of immersion took place. Again, there is no consensus among scholars as to how John baptized. Similar to the Qumranians of his time, John may have used one of the three types of immersion when he baptized.

Initiatory

Perhaps it would be well to point out that there are two types of washing purifications or baptisms. One is initiatory. It is a rite required of someone who wishes to enter a group. It does not have to be repeated. The second is a rite that is repeated at intervals as a sign of purification from evil thoughts, words or deeds.

From the translations of Brownlee and Vermes and the opinions of several scholars like Burrows, the Qumranian "baptisms" were probably initiatory in the sense that they were repeatable. The Qumran community was careful to avoid any type of defilement. Therefore, one of their major concerns was the laws of purification. It seems reasonable to assume that the Manual of Discipline (6:14-23) had to do with requirements for admission into the Qumran community. However, the Manual of Discipline (3:4-9; 5:13-14) seems to refer to the neophyte and lapsed members of the Qumran community. Scholars like Cross have suggested that all members of the community submitted themselves to baptisms once a year, probably on the feast of the renewal of the covenant. Since membership was restricted to Jews, the community was mindful of the convenant. Because the Qumranians believed that some Jews had rejected the laws of God, they demanded a renewal of dedication to the law through repentance. Therefore, it seems plausible to say that the Qumranian "baptisms" were repeatable.

On the other hand, John's baptism seems to have been a non-repeatable rite. This does not mean that John did not practice regular washings of the traditional type. Rather, the difference is one of emphasis. John seems to have stressed the need for once-for-all decision, 'that is, an abandonment of sin, and a life

47

befitting a member of the people of God. Matthew (3:2-3) states, "Repent for the Kingdom of Heaven is at hand." Luke's account (3:3-4) records, "He went into all the region about the Jordan, preaching a baptism of repentance for the forgiveness of sins." Mark's gospel (1:8) reads, "I have baptized you with water but he will baptize you with the Holy Spirit." These synoptic passages seem to indicate that John's baptism was non-repeatable and it was temporary. It was a preparation for another baptism that would be greater than his own. Luke's gospel (3:16-17) states, "I baptize you with water but he who is mightier than I is coming, the thong of whose sandals I am not worthy to untie; he will baptize you with the Holy Spirit and with Fire." Therefore, John's baptism was probably initiatory in the sense that it was non-repeatable.

A Baptism of Repentance

Both John's baptism and the Qumranian "baptism" seem to be identical in their view of repentance. The Manual of Discipline (3:4-6 B.V.) says, "He can not purify himself by atonement, nor cleanse with water for impurity, nor sanctify himself with seas or rivers, nor cleanse himself with any water for washing. Unclean! Unclean! shall he be as long as he rejects God's laws." Another passage of the Manual (3:8-9 B.V.) states, "through an upright and humble spirit that his sin will be atoned, and through the submission of his soul to all God's ordinances his flesh will be cleansed." These translations indicate that a moral purification, in addition to a physical purification, was demanded by the Qumranians. The need for repentance is interwoven in the Manual of Discipline. It seems probable that the Qumranian "baptism" was a baptism of repentance. It was more than a ritual ablution. One had to have a moral repentance of his sins before he was forgiven by God.

Likewise, the Synoptic Gospels indicate that John's baptism was a baptism of repentance. Mark's account (1:4-5) says, "Preaching a baptism of repentance for the forgiveness of sins." Luke's gospel (3:3-4) records, "He went into all the region about the Jordan, preaching a baptism of repentance for the forgiveness of sins." Matthew's account (3:11) reads, "I baptize you with water for repentance." All three synoptic accounts indicate that John's baptism was a baptism of repentance. Without the prior condition of repentance, apparently neither John nor the Qumranians would administer their baptism. On this point both seem to be in agreement.

CONCLUSIONS

In conclusion the importance of the Manual of Discipline, and the Synoptic Gospels needs no emphasis. The Manual of Discipline describes the Qumranian baptismal practices. The Manual of Discipline discusses the Qumranian moral washings. On the other hand, the synoptic accounts relate the baptismal practice of John the Baptist. From these writings, it is possible to reconstruct the religious rites and practices of the Qumranians and John the Baptist.

It is possible to make these conclusions:

1. Neither the Qumranians nor John the Baptist used a set formula in their baptismal practices.

2. John's use of the words "Holy Spirit" seems to be peculiar to him rather than to Qumranian dependence. However, the word Spirit is not peculiar to either John or the Qumranians. It stems from an older source, perhaps the book of Ezekiel.

3. Although the Manual of Discipline uses expressions such as "Community of his Council," "Council of the Community," "Purity of the Holy Men" and "Saints," the synoptic accounts do not. It may be assumed that John did not wish to identify his candidates with the Qumran community.

4. In their baptismal practices, the Qumranians and John used water but the condition of the water is not known. They baptized in the same general vicinity of the Jordan River, perhaps a few miles from one another. The recipients of their baptism were probably Jews. It is possible, however, that the broader mission of John may have touched both Jew and non-Jew. The Qumranians demanded a period of probation before baptizing a neophyte. There is no evidence that John followed this procedure. Both John the Baptist and the Qumranians are similar in their insistence on repentance before baptism, since they both shared the same eschatological outlook.

5. Apparently, John administered baptism while the Qumranians' baptism was self-administered. Although it is not clear how each administered their baptisms it seems likely that it was a type of immersion. Unlike the Qumranian "baptism," John's was probably a non-repeatable rite. The main difference between

these two baptisms seems to be that John's "baptism" was related
to the coming of Jesus and entry into a new community to be led
by Jesus. There is no reference in the Qumranian literature that
connects their baptisms with the Teacher of Righteousness or any
other figure.

6. Turning to the purpose of these baptisms, the Manual of
Discipline suggests that baptism marked entry into an eschatological community. Eschatology is the doctrine of the last days of
the world. It was an important belief of the Qumran community.
They believed that the prophets spoke of the last days and that
God had raised up a priestly teacher among them, who revealed
the mysteries which had been committed to the prophets and to
the community. They were conscious of living in expectation
of the end of the world. This belief, that the end was at hand,
guided their common life especially in their baptism rites.
The Manual of Discipline (3:4-0; 5:13-14) indicates that the
waters of cleansing, or water purifications, were not in themselves able to cleanse men from sin. Man had to repent of his
sins before he could receive forgiveness from God. No washing,
therefore, were of any avail without sincere repentance. The
Qumran baptism shows a drawing together of two ideas, ritual
or ceremonial defilement and moral failure.

This point calls to mind John's baptism of repentance for
the forgiveness of sins (Matthew 3:1-17; Mark 1:4-11; Luke 3:1-17).
John, like the Qumranians, expected the imminent beginning of a
new age. He speaks of another who will be greater than he and
who will baptize with the Holy Spirit and with Fire. (Matthew
3:11) John demanded a repentance, a turning from man's evil
ways to the ways of God. His emphasis is on moral cleanliness
rather than ritual purification. These two points show a close
affinity to the Qumran eschatology. Although John probably was
not a member of the Qumran community, he was a contemporary. He
preached and baptized in the general vicinity of Qumran. It
seems improbable that he was not aware of their existence.
His baptism rite is closer to the Qumranian "baptism" rite than
the Jewish proselyte baptism. However, John's eschatology differs
from that of the Qumranians on two points: John was preparing
people for the new age that would be started by Jesus; John
gives no indication that his baptism granted admission into a
sect or a monastic community. Therefore, the Qumranian "baptism"
and John's baptism indicate a more advanced type of baptism than
was in existence during that time.

7. The Qumran community was a sect closely organized under authoritative leaders. From their literature, it seems clear that they withdrew from normative Judaism and established a sectarian community. Separation from evil and wicked men was basic to the concept of the community. The member or the neophyte had to observe the strict laws of the Torah. It is clear that a neophyte was entering a community life. The question arises whether or not John the Baptist was establishing a new community with his baptism.

Brownlee's and Vermes' translations of the <u>Manual of Discipline</u> (3:4-9) use the term "Community of his Counsel." Brownlee (MD 6:14-23) uses the term "Council of the Community" while Vermes translates it "Council of the Congregation." In another passage of the <u>Manual of Discipline</u> (5:13), Brownlee uses the term "Purity of the Holy Men" and Vermes translates it as "Saints." All of these terms apparently refer to the full-fledged members of the Qumran community. The terms "Holy Men" and "Saints" apparently refer to the living members of the Community. From these passages, it seems that the neophytes were being baptized as members of this community.

However, the synoptic accounts do not indicate that John initiated neophytes into a new community. Several scholars hold that John was forming a new community. The synoptic accounts do not support their theory. Since the terms under discussion in this section are not mentioned in the snyoptic accounts, one interpretation might be that John wished to differentiate his followers from the Qumran community. Therefore, he would have avoided any term that could imply a Qumranian connection.

In final conclusion, the Qumranians and John the Baptist believed in an active God, the creator and judge of all men. In both, God demands the obedience of man, and the future rests in his hands. Both groups are convinced that they are living in the last days of the world. Both groups believed that the imminence of God demands immediate repentance by sinful man.

APPENDIX

MANUAL OF DISCIPLINE

William Brownlee's Translation of the Manual of Discipline[1]

Chapter 3:4-9

While in iniquity, he cannot be reckoned perfect
He cannot purify himself by atonement
Nor cleanse himself with water-for-impurity,
Nor sanctify himself with seas or rivers,
Nor cleanse himself with any water for washing!
Unclean! Unclean! shall he be as long as he rejects God's
laws so as not to be instructed by the Community of His
counsel. For it is through the spirit of God's true counsel
in regard to a man's ways that all his iniquities will be
atoned so that he may look upon the life-giving light, and
through a holy spirit disposed toward Unity in His Truth
that he will be cleansed of all his iniquities, and through an
upright and humble spirit that his sin will be atoned, and
through the submission of his soul to all God's ordinances
that his flesh will be cleansed so that he may purify himself with water-for-impurity and sanctify himself with rippling water.

Chapter 5:13-14

These may not enter into water to be permitted to touch
the Purity of the holy men, for they will not be cleansed
unless they have turned from their wickedness, for uncleanness clings to all transgressors of His word.

Chapter 6:14-23

And everyone from Israel who dedicates himself to
join the Council of the Community - the man who is Overseer at the head of the Many shall examine him as to his

---

[1] Brownlee, The Dead Sea Manual of Discipline, 12-26

understanding and his deeds. And if he grasps instruction,
he shall bring him into the covenant to turn to the truth and
to turn away from all perversity, and he shall enlighten him
in all the laws of the Community. Afterward, when he comes
to stand before the Many, the whole group will be asked
concerning his affairs; and however it is decided under God
in accordance with the counsel of the Many, he will either
draw near or draw away. But when he draws near the
Council of the Community, he must not touch the Purity
of the Many until they investigate him as to his spirit
and his deeds, until the completion of a full year by him.
Neither shall he share in the property of the Many; but
upon his completion of a year in the midst of the Community,
the Many shall be asked concerning his affairs with reference
to his understanding and his deeds in the Torah; and if it is
decided under God that he should draw near or, nearer the
Conclave of the Community, according to the judgment of
the priests and the majority of the men of their covenant,
his wealth and his property shall be conveyed to the man
who is Custodian of Property of the Many, and he shall enter it
to his credit, but shall not spend of it for the Many. He
the neophyte shall not touch the drink of the Many until
his completion of a second year among the men of the Community. But upon his completion of a second year, he the
Overseer shall examine him under the direction of the Many;
and if it is decided under God to admit him into the Community, he shall enroll him in the order of his assigned position among his brethren for Torah, and for judgment, and
for Purity, and to pool his property; and his counsel shall
belong to the Community, also his judgment.

Geza Vermes' Translation of the Manual of Discipline[2]

Chapter 3:4-9

He shall not be reckoned among the perfect;
he shall neither be purified by atonement,
nor cleansed by purifying waters,
nor sanctified by seas and rivers,
nor washed clean with any ablution.

---

[2] Vermes, The Dead Sea Scrolls in English, 74-82.

Unclean, unclean shall he be. For as
long as he despises the precepts of God
he shall receive no instruction in the
Community of His counsel.
For it is through the spirit of true counsel
concerning the ways of man that all his sins shall be
expiated that he may contemplate the light of life.
He shall be cleansed from all his sins
by the spirit of holiness uniting him to His truth,
and his iniquity shall be expiated by the
spirit of uprightness and humility.
And when his flesh is sprinkled with
purifying water and sanctified by cleansing water,
it shall be made clean by the humble submission
of his soul to all the precepts of God.

Chapter 5:13-14

They shall not enter the water to partake of
the pure Meal of the saints, for they shall not be cleansed
unless they turn from their wickedness: for
all who transgress His word are unclean.

Chapter 6:14-23

Every man, born of Israel, who freely pledges himself to
join the Council of the Community, shall be examined by the Guardian
at the head of the Congregation concerning his understanding and his
deeds. If he is fitted to the discipline, he shall admit him into
the Covenant that he may be converted to the truth and depart from
all falsehood; and he shall instruct him in all the rules of the
Community. And later, when he comes to stand before the Congregation, they shall all deliberate his case, and according to the decision of the Council of the Congregation he shall either enter or
depart. After he has entered the Council of the Community he shall
not touch the pure Meal of the Congregation until one full year is
completed, and until he has been examined concerning his spirit and
deeds; nor shall he have any share of the property of the Congregation. Then when he has completed one year within the Community, the
Congregation shall deliberate his case with regard to his understanding and observance of the Law. And if it be his destiny, according
to the judgment of the Priests and the multitude of the men of their
Covenant, to enter the company of the Community, his property and
earnings shall be handed over to the Bursar of the Congregation who

shall register it to his account and shall not spend it for the
Congregation. He shall not touch the Drink of the Congregation
until he has completed a second year among the men of the Community.
But when the second year has passed, he shall be examined, and if it
be his destiny, according to the judgment of the Congregation, to
enter the Community, then he shall be inscribed among his brethren
in the order of his rank for the Law, and for justice, and for the
pure Meal; his property shall be merged and he shall offer his counsel and judgment to the Community.

The New Testament of the Jerusalem Bible Translation of the Synoptic Gospels Account of John the Baptist's Baptism Rite

Matthew 3:1-17

(1) In due course John the Baptist appeared; he preached in the wilderness of Judaea and this was his message: (2) "Repent, for the kingdom of heaven is close at hand." (3) This was the man the prophet Isaiah spoke of when he said, "A voice cries in the wilderness: Prepare a way for the Lord, make his paths straight."

(4) This man John wore a garment made of camel-hair with a leather belt round his waist, and his food was locusts and wild honey. (5) Then Jerusalem and all Judaea (6) and the whole Jordan district made their way to him, and as they were baptised by him in the river Jordan they confessed their sins. (7) But when he saw a number of Pharisees and Sadducees coming for baptism he said to them, "Brood of vipers, who warned you to fly from the retribution that is coming? But (8) if you are repentant, produce the appropriate fruit, (9) and do not presume to tell yourselves, 'We have Abraham for our father,' because I tell you, God can raise children for Abraham from these stones. (10) Even now the axe is laid to the roots of the trees, so that any tree which fails to produce good fruit will be cut down and thrown on the fire. (11) I baptise you in water for repentance, but the one who follows me is more powerful than I am and I am not fit to carry his sandals; he will baptise you with the Holy Spirit and Fire. (12) His winnowing-fan is in his hand; he will clear his threshing-floor and gather his wheat into the barn; but the chaff he will burn in a fire that will never go out."

(13) Then Jesus appeared: he came from Galilee to the Jordan to be baptised by John. (14) John tried to dissuade him. "It is I who need baptism from you," he said, "and yet you come to me." (15) But Jesus replied, "Leave it like this for the time being it is fitting that we should, in this way, do all that righteousness demands." At this John gave in to him.

(16) As soon as Jesus was baptised he came up from the water, and suddenly the heavens opened and he saw the Spirit of God descending like a dove and coming down on him. And a voice spoke from heaven, "This is my Son, the Beloved; my favor rests on him."

Mark 1:4-11

(4) And so it was that John the Baptist appeared in the wilderness, proclaiming a baptism of repentance for the forgiveness of sins. (5) All Judaea and all the people of Jerusalem made their way to him, and as they were baptised by him in the river Jordan they confessed their sins. (6) John wore a garment of camel-skin, and he lived on locusts and wild honey. (7) In the course of his preaching he said, "Someone is following me, someone who is more powerful than I am, and I am not fit to kneel down and undo the strap of his sandals. (8) I have baptised you with water, but he will baptise you with the Holy Spirit."

(9) It was at this time that Jesus came from Nazareth in Galilee and was baptised in the Jordan by John. (10) No sooner had he come up out of the water than he saw the heavens torn apart and the Spirit, like a dove, descending on him, (11) and a voice came from heaven, "You are my Son, the Beloved; my favour rests on you."

Luke 3:1-22

(1) In the fifteenth year of Tiberius Caesar's reign, when Pontius Pilate was governor of Judaea, Herod tetrarch of Galilee, his brother Philip tetrarch of the lands of Ituraea and Trachonitis, Lysanias tetrarch of Abilene, (2) during the pontificate of Annas and Caiaphas, the word of God came to John son of Zechariah, in the wilderness. (3) He went through the whole Jordan district proclaiming a baptism of repentance for the forgiveness of sins, (4) as it is written in the book of the sayings of the prophet Isaiah: "A voice cries in the wilderness: Prepare a way for the Lord, make his paths straight. (5) Every valley will be filled in, every mountain and hill be laid low, winding ways will be straightened and rough roads made smooth. (6) And all mankind shall see the salvation of God."

(7) He said, therefore, to the crowds who came to be baptised by him, "Brood of vipers, who warned you to fly from the retribution that is coming? (8) But if you are repentant, produce the

appropriate fruits, and do not think of telling yourselves, 'We have Abraham for our father' because, I tell you, God can raise children for Abraham from these stones. (9) Yes, even now the axe is laid to the roots of the trees, so that any tree which fails to produce good fruit will be cut down and thrown on the fire."

(10) When all the people asked him, "What must we do, then?" (11) He answered "If anyone has two tunics he must share with the man who has none, and the one with something to eat must do the same." (12) There were tax collectors too who came for baptism, and these said to him, "Master, what must we do?" (13) He said to them, "Exact no more than your rate." (14) Some soldiers asked him in their turn, "What about us? What must we do?" He said to them, "No intimidation! No extortion! Be content with your pay!"

(15) A feeling of expectancy had grown among the people, who were beginning to think that John might be the Christ, (16) so John declared before them all, "I baptise you with water, but someone is coming, someone who is more powerful than I am, and I am not fit to undo the strap of his sandals; he will baptise you with the Holy Spirit and Fire. (17) His winnowing-fan is in his hand to clear his threshing-floor and to gather the wheat into his barn; but the chaff he will burn in a fire that will never go out." (18) As well as this, there were many other things he said to exhort the people and to announce the Good News to them.

(19) But Herod the the tetrarch, whom he criticized for his relations with his brother's wife Herodias and for all the other crimes Herod had committed, (20) added a further crime to all the rest by shutting John up in prison.

(21) Now when all the people had been baptised and while Jesus after his own baptism was at prayer, heaven opened (22) and the Holy Spirit descended on him in bodily shape, like a dove. And a voice came from heaven, "You are my Son, the Beloved; my favour rests on you."

Matthew 3:1-17

In those days came John the Baptist, preaching in the wilderness
of Judea
"Repent, for the kingdom of heaven is at hand."
For this is he who was spoken of by the prophet Isaiah when he
said, "The voice of one crying in the wilderness; Prepare the
way of the Lord, make his paths straight."
Now John wore a garment of camel's hair, and a leather girdle
around his waist; and his food was locusts and wild honey.
Then went out to Him Jerusalem and all Judea and all the region
about the Jordan,
and they were baptized by him in the river of Jordan, confessing
their sins.
But when he saw many of the Pharisees and Sadducees coming for
baptism, he said to them, "You brood of vipers! Who warned you
to flee from the wrath to come?
Bear fruit that befits repentance,
and do not presume to say to yourselves, 'We have Abraham as our
father'; for I tell you, God is able from these stones to raise
up children to Abraham.
Even now the axe is laid to the root of the trees; every tree
therefore that does not bear good fruit is cut down and thrown
into the fire.
"I baptize you with water for repentance, but he who is coming
after me is mightier than I, whose sandale I am not worthy to
carry; he will baptize you with the Holy Spirit and with fire.
His winnowing fork is in his hand, and he will clear his threshing floor and gather his wheat into the granary, but the chaff
will burn will unquenchable fire."
Then Jesus came from Gagilee to the Jordan to John, to be baptized by him.
John would have prevented him, saying, "I need to be baptized
by you, and do you come to me?"
But Jesus answered him, "Let it be so now; for thus it is fitting
for us to fulfill all righteousness." Then he consented.
And when Jesus was baptized, he went up immediately from the
water, and behold, the heavens were opened and he saw the Spirit
of God descending like a dove, and alighting on him;
and lo, a voice from heaven, saying, "This is my beloved Son,
with whom I am well pleased."

John the baptizer appeared in the wilderness, preaching a bap-
tism of repentance for the forgiveness of sins.
And there went out to him all the country of Judea, and all the
people of Jerusalem; and they were baptized by him in the river
Jordan, confessing their sins.
Now John was clothed with camel's hair, and had a leather girdle
around his waist and ate locusts and wild soney.
And he preached, saying "after me comes he who is mightier than
I, the thong of whose sandals I am not worthy to stoop down and
untie.
I have baptized you with water; but he will baptize you with
the Holy Spirit."
In those days Jesus came from Nazareth of Galilee and was baptized by John in the Jordan.
And when he came up out of the water, immediately he saw the
heavens opened and the Spirit descending upon him like a dove;
and a voice came from heaven, "Thou art my beloved Son; with
thee I am well pleased."

Luke 3:1-22

In the fifteenth year of the reign of Tiberius Caesar, Pontius
Pilate being governor of Judea, and Herod being tetrarch of
Galilee, and his brother Philip tetrarch of the region of
Ituraea and Trachonitis and Lysanias tetrarch of Abilene,
in the high-priesthood of Annas and Caiaphas, the word of God
came to John the son of Zechariah in the wilderness;
and he went into all the region about the Jordan, preaching a
baptism of repentance for the forgiveness of sins.
As it is written in the book of the words of Isaiah the prophet,
"The voice of one crying in the wilderness: Prepare the way of
the Lord, make his paths straight.
Every valley shall be filled, and every mountain and hill shall
be brought low, and the crooked shall be made straight, and the
rough ways shall be made smooth;
and all flesh shall see the salvation of God."
He said therefore to the multitudes that came out to be baptized
by him, "You brood of vipers! Who warned you to flee from the
wrath to come?
Bear fruits that befit repentance, and do not begin to say to
yourselves, 'We have Abraham as our father'; for I tell you,
God is able from these stones to raise up children to Abraham.

Even now the axe is laid to the root of the trees; every tree
therefore that does not bear good fruit is cut down and thrown
into the fire."
And the multitude asked him, "What then shall we do?"
And he answered them, "He who has two coats, let him share with
him who has none; and he who has good, let him do likewise."
Tax collectors also came to be baptized, and said to him,
"Teacher, what shall we do?"
And he said to them, "Collect no more than is appointed you."
Soldiers also asked him, "And we, what shall we do?" and he
said to them, "Rob no one by violence or by false accusation,
and be content with your wages."
As the people were in expectation, and all men questioned in
their hearts concerning John, whether perhaps he were the Christ.
John answered them all, "I baptize you with water; but he who is
mightier than I is coming, the thong of whose sandals I am not
worthy to untie; he will baptize you with the Holy Spirit and
with Fire.
His winnowing fork is in his hand, to clear his threshing floor,
and to gether the wheat into his granary, but the chaff he will
burn with unquenchable fire."
So, with many other exhortations, he preached good news to the
people.
But Herod the tetrarch, who had been reproved by him for Herodias,
his brother's wife, and for all the evil things that Herod had
done
added this to them all, that he shut up John in prison.
Now when all the people were baptized, and when Jesus also had
been baptized and was praying, the heaven was opened,
and the Holy Spirit descended upon him in bodily form, as a dove,
and a voice came from heaven, "Thou art my beloved Son, with thee
I am well pleased."

FOOTNOTES

1   Cecil Roth, The Historical Background of the Dead Sea Scrolls, New York: Philosophical Library, Inc., 1959, 23-52.

2   Geoffrey Driver, The Judaean Scrolls, New York: Schocken Books, Inc., 1965, 266-284.

3   Louis Finkelstein, ed., The Jews, Their History, Culture and Religion, 2 vols., New York: Harper and Brothers, 1960, 1, 136-140.

4   D. S. Russell, Between the Testaments, Philadelphia: Fortress Press, 1965, 54.

5   John Bright, A History of Israel, Philadelphia: The Westminster Press, MCMLIX, 450.

6   John E. Pryke, "Beliefs and Practices of the Qumran Community," The Church Quarterly Review, July-September, 1967, 168:318.

7   Millar Burrows, The Dead Sea Scrolls, New York: The Viking Press, 1955, 172.

8   W. D. Davies, Introduction to Pharisaism, Philadelphia: Fortress Press, 1967, 17-24.

9   William H. Brownlee, The Meaning of the Qumran Scrolls for the Bible, New York: Oxford University Press, 1964, 58-59.

10   Edmund Sutcliffe, The Monks of Qumran, Maryland: The Newman Press, 1960, 16-18.

11   Frank Moore Cross, Jr., The Ancient Library of Qumran and Modern Biblical Studies, Revised Edition, Garden City, New York: Doubleday and Company, Inc., 1961, 53-54.

12   Jozef T. Milik, Ten Years of Discovery in the Wilderness of Judea, Studies in Biblical Theology, No. 26, J. Strugnell, trans., London: SCM Press Ltd., 1959, 11.

13   M. H. Bresslau, <u>Hebrew and English Dictionary</u>, London: Crosby Lockwood and Son, 1913, 303-304.

14   Ludwig Koehler and Walter Baumgartner, eds., <u>Lexicon in Veteris Testamenti Libros</u>, Leiden, Netherlands: E. J. Brill, 1953, 495.

15   C. C. McCown, "The Scene of John's Ministry and Its Relation to the Purpose and Outcome of his Mission," <u>Journal of Biblical Literature</u>, LIX, 113.

16   Robert Funk, "The Wilderness," <u>Journal of Biblical Literature</u>. 1959, 78, 205-214.

17   Milik, 50-54; Stauffer, <u>Jesus and the Wilderness Community at Qumran</u>. 1-2.

18   J. Van Der Ploeg, <u>The Excavations at Qumran</u>, Kevin Smyth, trans., New York: Longmans, Green and Co., 1958, 62-68.

19   Roth, <u>The Historical Background of the Dead Sea Scrolls</u>, 3-6.

20   Finkelstein, ed., <u>The Jews, The History, Culture and Religion</u>, I, 134-135.

21   Burrows, <u>The Dead Sea Scrolls</u>, 245.

22   Millar Burrows, <u>More Light on the Dead Sea Scrolls</u>, New York: The Viking Press, 1958, 56-57.

23   Andres Fernandez, <u>The Life of Christ</u>, Paul Barrett, trans., Westminister, Maryland: The Newman Press, 1958, 22-24.

24   Ibid., 24: Ferdinand Prat, <u>Jesus Christ</u>, 2 vols., John Heenan, trans., Milwaukee, Wisconsin: The Bruce Publishing Co., 1959, 1, 488.

25   William LaSor, <u>The Dead Sea Scrolls and the New Testament</u>, Grand Rapids, Michaign: William B. Eerdmans, 1972, 143.

26   Prat, 1, 342-344

27   Geoffrey Driver, <u>The Judaean Scrolls</u>, New York: Schocken Books, 1965, 491-494.

28   Fernandez, 402.

29   John L. McKenzie, _Dictionary of the Bible_, Milwaukee,
Wisconsin: The Bruce Publishing Company, 1965, 195.

30   Fernandez, 71.

31   Prat, 1, 145-146.

32   John Steinmueller and Kathryn Sullivan, eds. _Catholic
Biblical Encyclopedia Old and New Testaments_. New York:
Joseph F. Wagner, Inc., 1956.

33   McKenzie, "The Gospel According to Matthew," in Brown,
Fitzmer, and Murphy, eds., Section 43, 23, 68.

34   McCown, "The Scene of John's Ministry and Its Relation
to the Purpose and Outcome of His Mission," _Journal of Biblical
Literature_, 1940, LIX, 113.

35   C. W. Wilson, "The Wilderness of Judaea," in James
Hastings, ed., _A Dictionary of the Bible_, 4 vols., New York:
Charles Scribner's Sons, 1908, 2, 792.

36   Isaac Landman, ed., "Wilderness," _The Universal Jewish
Encyclopedia_, 10 vols., New York: KTAV Publishing House, Inc.,
1969, 10, 519.

37   Cecil Roth and Geoffrey Wigoder, eds., "Wilderness,"
Encyclopedia Judaica, 16 vols., New York: The Macmillan Co.,
1972, 16, 512.

38   W. H. Brownlee, "John the Baptist in the New Light of
Ancient Scrolls," in Krister Stendahl, ed., _The Scrolls and the
New Testament_, New York: Harper and Brothers, 1957, 34.

39   Steinmueller and Sullivan, eds., Section 2, 358.

40   Jean Danielou, _The Work of John the Baptist_, Joseph Horn,
trans., Baltimore, Maryland: Helicon Press, Inc. 1966, 38.

41   Driver, 491-494.

42   Robert North and Raymond Brown, "Biblical Geography," in Brown, Fitzmyer, and Murphy, eds., Section 73, 648.

43   Oscar Cullman, "The Significance of the Qumran Texts for Research into the Beginnings of Christianity," _Journal of Biblical Literature_, 1955, LXXIV, 219.

44   Jean Steinmann, _Saint John the Baptist and the Desert Tradition_, Michael Boyes, trans., London: Longmans, Green and Co., Inc., 1958, 59.

45   Jean Danielou, _The Dead Sea Scrolls and Primitive Christianity_, Salvator Attanasio, trans., Baltimore, Maryland: Helicon Press, Inc., 1958, 18.

46   LaSor, 143.

47   Hans Conzelmann, _The Theology of St. Luke_, Geoffrey Buswell, trans., New York: Harper and Row, Publishers, 1960, 25.

48   A. Dupont Sommer, _The Jewish Sect of Qumran and the Essenes_, R.D. Barnett, trans., New York: The Macmillan Co., 1956, 149.

49   John A. Robinson, "The Baptism of John and the Qumran Community," _Harvard Theological Studies_, 1957, 50, 177.

50   John Pryke, "John the Baptist and the Qumran Community," _Revue de Qumran_, April, 1964, 4, 486.

51   F. F. Bruce, _The New Testament_, London: Thomas Nelson and Sons, Ltd., 1969, 146.

52   R. K. Harrison, _The Dead Sea Scrolls_, New York: Harper and Row Publishers, 1961, 108-109.

53   Charles H. Scobie, "John the Baptist," _The Scrolls and Christianity_, Matthew Black, ed., London: The Talbot Press, 1969, 58, 66.

54   John A. Robinson, "The Baptism of John and the Qumran Community," _Harvard Theological Studies_, 1957, 50, 176-177.

55   Oscar Cullmann, "The Significance of the Qumran Texts for Research into the beginnings of Christianity," _Journal of Biblical Literature_, 1955, LXXIV, 219.

56   John Allegro, The Dead Sea Scrolls and the Origins of Christianity, New York: Criterior Books, 1967, 164.

57   Brownlee, "John the Baptist in the New Light of Ancient Scrolls," Interpretation, 1955, 9, 71-73.

58   Lucretta Mowry, The Dead Sea Scrolls and the Early Church, Chicago: University of Chicago, 1962, 134.

59   Kurt Schubert, The Dead Sea Community: Its Origin and Teachings, London: Adam and Charles Black, Ltd., 1959, 126, 131.

60   Danielou, The Dead Sea Scrolls and Primitive Christianity, 16.

61   Steinmann, 60.

62   Jack Finegan, Light from the Ancient Past, Princeton, New Jersey: Princeton University Press, 1959, 293.

63   Raymond E. Brown, "Second Thoughts, the Dead Sea Scrolls and the New Testament," The Expository Times, October, 1966, LXXVIII, 19-23.

64   H. H. Rowley, The Dead Sea Scrolls and the New Testament, London: The Talbot Press, 1964, 15.

65   John Heron, "The Theology of Baptism," Scottish Journal of Theology, 1955, 8, 40.

66   Charles Fritsch, The Qumran Community, New York: The Macmillan Co., 1956, 113-114.

67   Burrows, More Light on the Dead Sea Scrolls, 56.

68   Pierre Benoit, "Qumran and the New Testament," in Jerome Murphy-O'Connor, ed., Paul and Qumran, Chicago, Illinois: The Priory Press, 6.

69   Cross, Jr., The Ancient Library of Qumran and Modern Biblical Studies, 204, note 9.

70   Cyrus Gordon, Adventures in the Nearest East, London: Phoenix House, Ltd., 1957, 135-136.

71   Edmund F. Sutcliffe, <u>The Monks of Qumran</u>, Westminster, Maryland: The Newman Press, 124.

72   Ethelbert Stauffer, <u>Jesus and the Wilderness Community at Qumran</u>, Hans Spalteholz, trans., Philadelphia, Pennsylvania: Fortress Press, 1964, 7.

73   Paul Heinish, <u>Theology of the Old Testament</u>, Wm. Heidt, trans., Collegeville, Minnesota: The Liturgical Press, 1955, 218-219.

74   Roland De Vaux, <u>Ancient Israel</u>, 2 vols., New York: McGraw-Hill, Inc., 1961, 2, 460-461.

75   Hugh Hahn, "Baptism," in Isaac Landman, ed., <u>The Universal Jewish Encyclopedia</u>, 10 vols., New York: KTAV Publishing House, Inc., 1969, 1, 68.

76   Schubert, 54-55.

77   Ringgren, 125.

78   Vermes, <u>The Dead Sea Scrolls in English</u>, 45.

79   Sutcliffe, <u>The Monks of Qumran</u>, 108-109.

80   Cross, Jr., 95, note 96a.

81   De Vaux, <u>Archaeology and the Dead Sea Scrolls</u>, 131-132.

82   Brownlee, "John the Baptist in the New Light of Ancient Scrolls," 39.

83   Cross, Jr., 67-68.

84   Sutcliffe, <u>The Monks of Qumran</u>, 26-28.

85   Milik, 56.

86   Driver, 43.

87   Fritsch, 5-8.

88   Cross, Jr., 68.

89   Allegro, 100.

90   Helmer Ringgren, *The Faith of Qumran*, Emilie T. Sander, trans. Philadelphia, Pennsylvania: Fortress Press, 1963, 222.

91   Cyrus H. Gordon, *Adventures in the Nearest East*, London: Phoenix House Ltd., 1957, 136.

92   Roth and Wigoder, 2, 82.

93   Sutcliffe, *The Monks of Qumran*, 108.

94   *Ibid.*

95   Roth and Wigoder, eds., "Ablutions," 2, 82.

96   *Ibid.*

97   Cecil Roth and Geoffrey Wigoder, eds., "Mikveh," *Encyclopedia Judaica*, 16 vols., New York: The Macmillan Co., 1972, 11, 1534.

98   *Ibid.*, 1534-1535.

99   Isaac Landman, ed., "Mikveh," *The Universal Jewish Encyclopedia*, New York: KTAV Publishing House Inc., 1969, 2, 108.

100   Cross, Jr., 67, Note 23, 234.

101   J. M'Clintock and J. Strong, eds., "Lustration," *Cyclopaedia of Biblical, Theological and Ecclesiastical Literature*, 10 vols., New York: Arno Press, 1969, 563-564. Lustration or bathing is a rite performed by a person on himself.

102   M'Clintock and Strong, eds., "Lustrations," 5, 563-565.

102   Cross, Jr., 67, note 23, 234.

103   Sutcliffe, *The Monks of Qumran*, 108-109.

104   Matthew Blcak, *The Scrolls and Christian Origins*, New York: Charles Scribner's Sons, 1961, 97.

105   Martin A. Larson, *The Essene Heritage*, New York: Philosophical Library, 1967, 130. Baptism is a rite performed by one person on another.

106   Isidore Singer, ed., "Baptism," The Jewish Encyclopedia, 12 vols., New York: KTAV Publishing House, Inc., 1901, 2, 499-500.

107   Albrecht Oepke, "The Meaning of Baptism," in Gerland Kittel, ed., Theological Dictionary of the New Testament, 9 vols., Grand Rapids, Michigan: William B. Eerdmans Publishing Company, 1965, 1, 529-537.

108   M'Clintock and Strong, eds., "Jewish Baptism," 1, 644.

109   Fritsch, 64-67.

110   Vermes, The Dead Sea Scrolls in English, 45.

111   Sutcliffe, The Monks of Qumran, 108.

112   Schubert, 54-55.

113   McKenzie, Dictionary of the Bible, 79.

114   Dupont-Sommer, 98-99.

115   J. Van Der Ploeg, The Excavations at Qumran, Kevin Smyth, trans., New York: Longmans, Green and Company, 1958, 211-212.

116   LaSor, 70.

117   Ringgren, 220.

118   Stauffer, 13.

119   Kevin Smyth, The Dead Sea Scrolls, London: Catholic Truth Society, 1956, 22.

120   De Vaux, Archaeology and the Dead Sea Scrolls, 132.

121   William F. Albright, From the Stone Age to Christianity, Garden City, New York: Doubleday and Co., Inc., 1957, 375-377.

122   Pierre Benoit, "Qumran and the New Testament," 7.

123   Salo Baron and Joseph Blau, Judaism, New York: Harper and Row Publishers, Inc., 1954, 78.

124   Harrison, 109-116.

125   Roland E. Murphy, The Dead Sea Scrolls and the Bible,
Maryland: The Newman Press, 1957, 65.

126   Rowley, The Dead Sea Scrolls and the New Testament, 222-223.

127   Cross, Jr., 95-96, note 96a, 234.

128   Steinmann, 60-69.

129   Robinson, "The Baptism of John and the Qumran Community,"
181-191.

130   Cullman, "The Significance of the Qumran Texts for Research
into the Beginnings of Christianity," 219.

131   Matthew Black, The Scrolls and Christian Origins, New
York: Charles Scribner's Sons, 1961, 98.

132   A.R.C. Leaney, The Rule of Qumran and Its Meaning,
Philadelphia, Pennsylvania: The Westminster Press, 1966, 142.

133   Ernest G. Wright, Biblical Archaeology, Philadelphia,
Pennsylvania: The Westminster Press, 1960, 155-156.

134   Gordon, 136.

135   John Heron, "The Theology of Baptism," Scottish Journal
of Theology, 1955, 8, 39.

136   Driver, 506.

137   Jack Finnegan, Light from the Ancient Past, Princeton,
New Jersey: Princeton University Press, 1959, 290.

138   Milik, 103.

139   Brown, "The Dead Sea Scrolls and the New Testament," 4.

140   Brownlee, "John the Baptist in the New Light of Ancient
Scrolls," 76-78.

141   Pryke, "John the Baptist and the Qumran Community," 489-496.

142   Allegro, 106-121.

143   G. R. Beasley-Murray, _Baptism in the New Testament_, Grand
Rapids, Michigan: William B. Eerdmans Publishing Co., 1962, 18.

144   Burrows, _More Light on the Dead Sea Scrolls_, 372.

145   Driver, 55-57.

146   Scholars like Burrows, Schubert, Milik, LaSor, Cross,
and Sutcliffe are noncommital about the word "touch."

146   Burrows, _More Light on the Dead Sea Scrolls_, 360-362.

147   LaSor, 50.

148   J. Delorme, "The Practice of Baptism in Judaism at the
Beginning of the Christian Era," in A. George, J. Delorme, D. Mollat,
J. Guillet, M. E. Boismard, J. Duplacy, J. Giblet, and Y. B. Tremel,
Baptism in the New Testament, David Askew, trans., London: Geoffrey
Chapman, 1964, 42-43.

149   McKenzie, _Dictionary of the Bible_, 714.

150   Schubert, 55.

151   Leaney, 172.

152   Brownlee, "BMD," 23, note 2.

153   Vermes, _The Dead Sea Scrolls in English_, 27.

154   Pryke, 494.

155   Baron and Blau, 78.

156   LaSor, 71.

157   Rowley, "The Baptism of John and the Qumran Sect," in
Higgins, 220; H. H. Rowley, "The Qumran Sect and Christian
Origins," _Bulletin of the John Ryland's Library_, 1961-1962, XLIV, 141.

158   Sutcliffe, _The Monks of Qumran_, 106.

159   Brownlee, "BMD," 25, note 33.

160   Milik, 102-103.

161   Rowley, "The Baptism of John and the Qumran Sect," in Higgins, ed., 219.

162   Sutcliffe, The Monks of Qumran, 105-106.

163   Leaney, 194-195.

164   LaSor, 71.

165   Pryke, "John the Baptist and the Qumran Community," 494; Pryke, "The Sacraments of Holy Baptism and Holy Communion in the Light of the Ritual Washings and Sacred Meals at Qumran," 544.

166   Brownlee, "BMD," 27, note 43.

167   Vermes, The Dead Sea Scrolls in English, 27.

168   Sutcliffe, The Monks of Qumran, 16.

169   LaSor, 35.

170   Burrows, More Light on the Dead Sea Scrolls, 21.

171   LaSor, 40-41.

172   Cross, Jr., 60-61.

173   Solomon Zeitlin, "The Hewbre Scrolls and the Status of Biblical Scholarship," Jewish Quarterly Review, 1951, 42, 133-192; Solomon Zeitlin, "The Dead Sea Scrolls: A travesty on Scholarship," Jewish Quarterly Review, 1956-1957, XLVII, 1-36.

174   LaSor, 42.

175   Burrows, More Light on the Dead Sea Scrolls, 56-57.

176   Werner G. Kummel, Introduction to the New Testament, A. J. Mattill, Jr., trans., Nashville, Tennessee: Abingdon Press, 1966, 31.

177   Steinmueller and Sullivan, eds., Section 2, 268.

178   McKenzie, *Dictionary of the Bible*, 254.

179   Steinmueller and Sullivan, eds., Section 2, 614.

180   Frederick Gast, "Synoptic Problem," in Raymond E. Brown, James A. Fitzmyer, and Roland E. Murphy, eds., *The Jerome Biblical Commentary*, Engelwood Cliffs, New Jersey: Prentice-Hall, Inc., 1968, Section 40, 1-2.

181   J. M'Clintock and J. Strong, eds., "Rite," *Cyclopaedia of Biblical, Theological and Ecclesiastical Literature*, X Vols., New York: Arno Press, 1969, IX, 35.

182   *Ibid.*

183   Edmund F. Sutcliffe, "Baptism and Baptismal Rites at Qumran," *Heythrop Journal*, 1960, 1, 185.

184   C. Ernst, ed., "Sacrament," *Concise Theological Dictionary* Richard Strachan, trans., Freiburg, Germany: Herder, 1965, 415.

185   P. Parente, A. Piolanti, and S. Garofalo, *Dictionary of Dogmatic Theology*, E. Doronzo, trans., Milwaukee, Wisconsin: The Bruce Publishing Co., 1957, 248.

186   Sutcliffe, "Baptism and Baptismal Rites at Qumran," *Heythrop Journal*, 1960, I, 185.

187   Harrison, *The Dead Sea Scrolls*, 115.

188   McKenzie, *Dictionary of the Bible*, 754.

189   Ethelbert W. Bullinger, *A Critical Lexicon and Concordance to the English and Greek Testament*, London: Samuel Bagster and Sons Ltd., 1969, 80.

190   *Ibid.*, 80-81.

191   Louis Boyer, *Dictionary of Theology*, Charles Quinn, trans., New York: Desclee Co., Inc., 1965, 51.

192   Hans Conzelmann, *An Outline of the Theology of the New Testament*, John Bowden, trans., New York: Harper and Row, Publishers, 1969, 47.

193   F. L. Cross, ed., <u>The Oxford Dictionary of the Christian</u>
<u>Church</u>. London: Oxford University Press, 1963, 124-125; Isaac
Landman, ed., <u>The Universal Jewish Encyclopedia</u>, 10 vols., New
York: KTAV Publishing House Inc., 1969, 3, 68.

194   M'Clintock and Strong, eds., I, 639-640.

195   Leon-DuFour, ed., <u>Dictionary of Biblical Theology</u>, 28-29.

196   Singer, ed., "Baptism," <u>The Jewish Encyclopedia</u>, 2, 499-500.

197   Sutcliffe, "Baptism and Baptismal Rites at Qumran," 180.

198   Rudolf Bultmann, <u>Jesus and the Word</u>, Louise Smith and
Ermine Lantero, trans., London: Collins Clear-Type Press, 1958, 26.

199   Ethelbert Stauffer, <u>New Testament Theology</u>, John Marsh,
trans., London: SCM Press Ltd., 1963, 22.

200   Robinson, "The Baptism of John and the Qumran Community,"
189

201   Steinmann, 66.

202   Edmund Schlink, <u>The Doctrine of Baptism</u>, Herbert J. Bouman,
trans., St. Louis, Missouri: Concordia Publishing House, 1972, 17-20.

203   Conzelmann, <u>An Outline of the Theology of the New Testament</u>, 48.

204   Berkeley Collins, "The Sacrament of Baptism in the New
Testament," <u>The Expository Times</u>, 1915, XXVII, 39.

205   Leonhard G. Goppelt, "In the New Testament," in G. Kittel
and G. Bromiley, eds., 1, 329.

206   Delorme, "The Practice of Baptism in Judaism at the beginning
of the Christian Era," in George <u>et al</u>., 54-55.

207   Scobie, "John the Baptist," in Black, ed., 61.

208   Brownlee, "John the Baptist in the New Light of Ancient
Scrolls," 43.

209   <u>Ibid</u>., 81.

210   <u>Ibid</u>., 42.

211   Thomas F. Torrance, "Aspects of Baptism in the New Testament," _Theologische Zeitschrift_, July-August, 1958, 14, 241.

212   David Stanley and Raymond Brown, "Aspects of New Testament Thought," in Brown, Fitzmyer, and Murphy, eds., Section 78, 780-781.

213   Leon-DuFour, _Dictionary of Biblical Theology_, 29.

214   Moore, I. 333; Clifton J. Allen, ed., _The Broadman Bible Commentary: General Articles Matthew-Mark_, 12 vols., Nashville Tennessee: Broadman Press, 1969, 8, 267; Clifton J. Allen, ed., _The Broadman Commentary: General Articles Luke-John_, 12 vols., Nashville, Tennessee: Broadman Press, 1969, 9, 92; William Flemington, "Baptism," _The Interpreter's Dictionary of the Bible_, 4 vols., New York: Abingdon Press, 1962, 1, 349.

215   .D. E. H. Whitely, _The Theology of St. Paul_, Philadelphia, Pennsylvania: Fortress Press, 1966, 167-168.

216   H. H. Rowley, "The Baptism of John and the Qumran Sect," in A. J. B. Higgins, ed., _New Testament Essays: Studies in Memory of Thomas W. Manson 1893-1958_, 1959, 223-228.

217   _Ibid_.

218   Gilmore, 74.

219   Fritsch, 114.

220   Allegro, 163.

221   Ringgren, 221, 243.

222   Boyer, 51.

223   Leon-DuFour, _Dictionary of Biblical Theology_, 29.

224   Roth and Wi goder, eds., _Encyclopaedia Judaica_, 2, 55-56.

225   Black, _The Scrolls and Christian Origins_, 97.

226   Jacques Guillet, _The Consciousness of Jesus_, Edmond Bobin, trans., New York: The Newman Press, 1972, 31-34.

227   Beasley-Murray, 40-42.

228   J. D. G. Dunn, "Spirit and Fire Baptism," _Novum Testamentum_, April, 1972, 2, 91-92.

229   Roland E. Murphy, _The Dead Sea Scrolls and the Bible_, Westminster, Maryland: The Newman Press, 1957, 61-65.

230   _Ibid._, 65.

231   _Ibid._

232   Harrison, _The Dead Sea Scrolls_, 109.

233   Oscar Cullmann, _Baptism in the New Testament_, Studies in Biblical Theology, I. J. D. Reid, trans., London: SCM Press Ltd., 1969, 219.

234   Conzelmann, _An Outline of the Theology of the New Testament_, 102.

235   Driver, 501-502.

236   Benoit, "Qumran and the New Testament," in Murphy-O'Connor, ed., 7-9.

237   LaSor, 150.

238   G. Kittel and G. Bromiley, eds., _Theological Dictionary of the New Testament_, 9 vols., G. Bromiley, trans., Grand Rapids, Michigan: William B. Eerdmans Publishing Co., 1965, 1, 537-538.

239   Brownlee, "John the Baptist in the New Light of Ancient Scrolls," 77.

240   Delorme, "The Practice of Baptism in Judaism at the Beginning of the Christian Era," in George, _et al._, 58-59.

241   Danielou, _The Work of John the Baptist_, 64-66.

242   Robinson, 180-184.

243   Schubert, 128-131.

244   Brown, "Second Thoughts on the Dead Sea Scrolls and
the New Testament," 19-23.

245   Burrows, More Light on the Dead Sea Scrolls, 60.

Books

Albright, William F. _The Archaeology of Palestine_. Baltimore,
Maryland: Penguin Books, 1954.

Albright, William F. _From the Stone Age to Christianity_.
Garden City, New York: Doubleday and Company, Inc., 1957.

Allegro, John M. _The Dead Sea Scrolls and the Origins of_
Christianity. New York: Criterion Books, 1967.

Allen, Clifton J., ed., _The Broadman Bible Commentary: General_
Articles Luke-John. 12 vols. Nashville, Tennessee:
Broadman Press, 1969.

Allen, Clifton J., ed., _The Broadman Bible Commentary: General_
Articles Matthew-Mark. 12 vols. Nashville, Tennessee:
Broadman Press, 1969.

Baron, Salo and Blau, Joseph. _Judaism_. New York: The Bobs-
Merrill Company, Inc., 1954.

Beasley-Murray, G. R., _Baptism in the New Testament_, Grand Rapids,
Michigan: William B. Eerdmans Publishing Company, 1962.

Black, Matthew. _The Scrolls and Christian Origins_. New York:
Charles Scribner's Sons, 1961.

Black, Matthew, ed. _The Scrolls and Christianity_. Theological
Collections II. London: The Talbot Press, 1969.

Boyer, Louis, _Dictionary of Theology_. Charles U. Quinn, trans.
New York: Desclee Company, Inc. 1965.

Bresslau, M. H. _Hebrew and English Dictionary_. London: Crosby
Lockwood and Son, 1913.

Bright, John. _A History of Israel_. Philadelphia, Pennsylvania:
The Westminster Press, 1959.

Brown, Raymond E. "The Dead Sea Scrolls and the New Testament,"
in James H. Charlesworth, ed. _John and Qumran_. London:
Geoffrey Chapman, 1972, 1-8.

Brown, Raymond E., Fitzmyer, James A., and Murphy, Roland E., eds., _The Jerome Biblical Commentary_. Englewood Cliffs, New Jersey: Prentice-Hall, Inc., 1968.

Brownlee, William H. "The Dead Sea Manual of Discipline: Translation and Notes," _Bulletin of the American Schools of Oriental Research_, Supplementary Studies Nos. 10-12. New Haven, Connecticut: American Schools of Oriental Research, 1951, 11-30.

Brownlee, William H. _The Meaning of the Qumran Scrolls for the Bible_. New York: Oxford University Press, 1964.

Bruce, F. F. _The New Testament History_. London: Thomas Nelson and Sons Ltd., 1969.

Burrows, Millar. _The Dead Sea Scrolls_. New York: The Viking Press, 1955.

Burrows, Millar. _More Light on the Dead Sea Scrolls_. New York The Viking Press, 1958.

Charlesworth, James H., ed. _John and Qumran_. London: Geoffrey Chapman, 1972.

Conzelmann, Hans. _An Outline of the Theology of the New Testament_. John Bowden, trans. New York: Harper and Row Publishers, 1969.

Cross, Jr., Frank Moore. _The Ancient Library of Qumran and Modern_ and Biblical Studies. Revised Edition. Garden City, New York: Doubleday and Company, Inc., 1961.

Cullman, Oscar. _Baptism in the New Testament_. Studies in Biblical Theology, I. J. K. Reid trans. London: SCM Press Ltd., 1969.

Danielou, Jean. _The Dead Sea Scrolls and Primitive Christianity_. Salvator Attanasio trans. Baltimore, Maryland: Helicon Press Inc., 1958.

Davies, A. Powell. _The Meaning of the Dead Sea Scrolls_. New York: The New American Library, 1956.

De Vaux, Roland. _Archaeology and the Dead Sea Scrolls_. London: Oxford University Press, 1973.

Driver, Geoffrey. _The Judean Scrolls_. New York: Schocken Books, Inc., 1965.

Dupont-Sommer, A. _The Jewish Sect of Qumran and the Essenes_. R. D. Barnett trans. New York: The MacMillan Company, 1956.

Fernandez, Andres. _The Life of Christ_. Paul Barrett, trans. Westminster, Maryland: The Newman Press, 1958.

Finegan, Jack. _Light from the Ancient Past_. Princeton, New Jersey: Princeton University Press, 1959.

Finkelstein, Louis, ed. _The Jews, Their Culture and Religion_. 2 vols. New York: Harper and Brothers, 1960.

Flusser, David. "The Dead Sea Sect and the Pre-Pauline Christianity," _Scripta Hierosolymitana_. 4 vols. C. Rabin and Y. Yadin eds., Jerusalem: The Magna Press, 1958, 4, 215-266.

Freedman, David and Greenfield, Jonas eds., _New Directions in Biblical Archaeology_. New York: Doubleday and Company, Inc., 1971.

Fritsch, Charles T. _The Qumran Community_. New York: The MacMillan Company, 1956.

George, A. Delorme, J., Mollat, D., Guillet, J., Boismard, M.E., Duplacy, J., Giblet, J., and Tremel, Y. H. _Baptism in the New Testament_. David Ashew, trans. London: Geoffrey Chapman, 1964.

Goppelt, Leonard G. "In the New Testament," _Theological Dictionary of the New Testament_. 9 vols. G. Kittel, and G. Bromiley, eds. G. Bromiley, trans. Grand Rapids, Michigan: William B. Eerdmans Publishing Company, 1963, I, 328-330.

Gordon, Cyrus H. _Adventures in the Nearest East_. London: Phoenix House Ltd., 1957.

Hahn, Hugh. "Baptism," _The Universal Jewish Encyclopedia_. 10 vols.
Isaac Landman, ed. New York: KTAV Publishing House Inc.,
1969, 1, 68-69.

Harrison, R. K. _The Dead Sea Scrolls_. New York: Harper and Row
Publishers, 1961.

Hastings, James, ed. _A Dictionary of the Bible_. 4 vols. New York:
Charles Scribner's Sons, 1903.

Kittel, G. and Bromiley G., eds. _Theological Dictionary of the
New Testament_. 9 vols. G. Bromiley, trans. Grand Rapids,
Michigan: William B. Eerdmans Publishing Company, 1965.

Kummel, Werner. Introduction to the New Testament. A. J.
Mattill, Jr., trans. Nashville, Tennessee: Abingdon Press,
1966.

Landman, Isaac, ed. _The Universal Jewish Encyclopedia_. 10 vols.
New York: KTAV Publishing House, Inc., 1969.

Landman, Isaac, ed. "Wilderness," _The Universal Jewish
Encyclopedia_. 10 vols. New York: KTAV Publishing House,
Inc., 1969, 10, 519-521.

LaSor, William. _The Dead Sea Scrolls and the New Testament_.
Grand Rapids, Michigan: William B. Eerdmans Publishing
Company, 1972.

Leaney, A. R. C. _The Rule of Qumran and Its Meaning_.
Philadelphia, Pennsylvania: The Westminster Press, 1966.

Leon-DuFour, Xavier. _Dictionary of Biblical Theology_.
P. J. Cahill, trans. New York: Desclee Company Inc.,
1967.

Lindblom, J. _Phrophecy in Ancient Israel_. Philadelphia,
Pennsylvania: Fortress Press, 1967.

M'Clintock, J. and Strong, J., eds. _Cyclopaedia of Biblical,
Theological and Ecclesiastical Literature_. 10 vols.
New York: Arno Press, 1969.

M'Clintock, J. and Strong, J., eds. "Lustrations," Cyclopaedia of Biblical, Theological and Ecclesiastical Literature, 10 vols, New York: Arno Press, 1969, V, 563-564.

M'Clintock, J. and Strong, J. "Rite," Cyclopaedia of Biblical, Theological and Ecclesiastical Literature. X, vols. New York: Arno Press, 1969, IX, 514-515.

McKenzie, John L. Dictionary of the Bible. Milwaukee, Wisconsin: The Bruce Publishing Company, 1965.

Milik, Josef T. Ten Years of Discovery in the Wilderness of Judea. Studies in Biblical Theology No. 26. J. Strugnell, trans. Naperville, Illinois: Alec R. Allenson Inc., 1959.

Moore, George Moore. Judaism. 3 vols. Cambridge, Massachusetts: Harvard University Press, 1962.

Mowry, Lucretta. The Dead Sea Scrolls and the Early Church. Chicago, Illinois: University of Chicago, 1962.

Murphy, Roland E. The Dead Sea Scrolls and the Bible. Westminster, Maryland: The Newman Press, 1957.

Parente, P., Piolanti, A., and Garofalo, S. Dictionary of Dogmatic Theology. E. Doronzo, trans. Milwaukee, Wisconsin: The Bruce Publishing Company, 1957.

Pfeiffer, Charles F. The Dead Sea Scrolls and the Bible. Grand Rapids, Michigan: Baker Book House, 1969.

Prat, Ferdinand. Jesus Christ. 2 vols. John Heenan, trans. Milwaukee, Wisconsin: The Bruce Publishing Company, 1959.

Rabin, Chaim. Qumran Studies. London: Oxford University Press, 1957.

Rengstorf, Karl H. Hirbet Qumran and the Problem of the Library of the Dead Sea Caves. Leiden, Netherlands: E. J. Brill, 1963.

Ringgren, Helmer. The Faith of Qumran. Emilie T. Sander, trans. Philadelphia, Pennsylvania: Fortress Press, 1963.

Roth, Cecil. _The Dead Sea Scrolls, A New Historical Approach_.
New York: W. W. Norton and Company, Inc., 1965.

Roth, Cecil. _The Historical Background of the Dead Sea Scrolls_.
New York: Philosophical Library Inc., 1959.

Roth, Cecil and Wigoder, Geoffrey, eds. _Encyclopedia Judaica_.
16 vols. New York: The MacMillan Company, 1972.

Roth, Cecil and Wigoder, Geoffrey, eds. "Wilderness,"
Encyclopedia Judaica. 16 vols. New York: The MacMillan
Company, 1972, 16, 512-514.

Rowley, H. H. _The Dead Sea Scrolls and the New Testament_. London:
The Talbot Press, 1964.

Russell, D. S. _Between the Testaments_. Philadelphia, Pennsylvania:
Fortress Press, 1965.

Schlink, Edmund. _The Doctrine of Baptism_. Herbert J. Bouman,
trans. St. Louis, Missouri: Conçordia Publishing House, 1972.

Schubert, Kurt. _The Dead Sea Community: Its Origin and Teachings_.
London: Adam and Charles Black Ltd., 1959.

Selby, Donald J. _Introduction to the New Testament_. New York:
The Macmillan Company, 1971.

Singer, Isaac, ed. "Baptism," _The Jewish Encyclopedia_. 12 vols.
New York: KTAV Publishing House Inc., 1901, 2, 499-500.

Singer, Isidore, ed. _The Jewish Encyclopedia_. 12 vols.
New York: KTAV Publishing House Inc., 1901.

Smyth, Kevin. _The Dead Sea Scrolls_. London: Catholic Truth
Society, 1956.

Stauffer, Ethelbert. _Jesus and the Wilderness Community at Qumran_.
Hans Spalteholz, trans. Philadelphia, Pennsylvania:
Fortress Press, 1964.

Steinmann, Jean. _Saint John the Baptist and the Desert Tradition_.
Michael Boyes, trans. London: Longmans, Green and Company
Ltd., 1958.

Steinmueller, John and Sullivan, Kathryn, eds. Catholic Biblical Encyclopedia Old and New Testament. New York: Joseph F. Wagner Inc., 1956.

Stendahl, Krister, ed. The Scrolls and the New Testament. New York: Harper and Brothers, 1957.

Sutcliffe, Edmund F. The Monks of Qumran. Westminster, Maryland: The Newman Press, 1960.

Van Der Ploeg, J. The Excavations at Qumran. Kevin Smyth, trans. New York: Longmans, Green and Company, 1958.

Vermes, Geza. The Dead Sea Scrolls in English. Baltimore, Maryland: Penguin Books, Inc., 1962.

Wilson, C. W. "The Wilderness of Judaea." A Dictionary of the Bible. 4 vols. James Hastings, ed. New York: Charles Scribner's Sons, 1903, 2, 792-794.

Wilson, Edmund. The Dead Sea Scrolls 1947-1969. New York: Oxford University Press, 1969.

Wright, G. Ernest. Biblical Archaeology. Abridged Edition. Philadelphia, Pennsylvania: The Westminster Press, 1960.

Yadin, Yigael. The Message of the Scrolls. New York: The University Press, 1962.

Zeitlin, Solomon. The Dead Sea Scrolls and Modern Scholarship. Philadelphia, Pennsylvania: Dropsie College, 1956.

Essays in Collections

Benoit, Pierre. "Qumran and the New Testament," in Jerome Murphy-O'Connor, ed. Paul and Qumran. Chicago, Illinois: The Priory Press 1968, 1-30.

Brownlee, William H. "John the Baptist in the Light of Ancient Scrolls," in Krister Stendahl, ed. The Scrolls and the New Testament. New York: Harper and Brothers, 1957, 33-53.

Delorme, J. "The Practice of Baptism in Judaism at the Beginning
of the Christian Era," in A. George, J. Delorme, D. Mollat,
J. Guillet, M. E. Boismard, J. Duplacy, and Y. B. Tremel.
Baptism in the New Testament. David Askew, trans. London:
Geoffrey Chapmann, 1964, 25-60.

Gast, Frederick. "Synoptic Problem," in Raymond E. Brown, James
A. Fitzmyer, and Roland E. Murphy, eds. The Jerome Biblical
Commentary. Englewood Cliffs, New Jersey: Prentice-Hall
Inc., 1968, Section 40, 2-6.

Harrison, R. K. "The Rites and Customs of the Qumran Sect," in
Matthew Black, ed. The Scrolls and Christianity. London:
The Talbot Press, 1969, 26-36.

North, Robert and Brown, Raymond. "Biblical Geography," in
R. Brown, J. Fitzmyer, and R. Murphy, eds. The Jerome
Biblical Commentary. Englewood Cliffs, New Jersey: Prentice-
Hall, Inc., Section 73, 633-652.

Rowley, H. H. "The Baptism of John and the Qumran Sect," in A. j. B.
Higgins, ed. The New Testament Essays: Studies in Memory of
Thomas W. Manson 1893-1958. Manchester: The University Press,
1959, 218-228.

Scobie, Charles H. "John the Baptist," in Matthew Black, ed. The
Scrolls and Christianity. London: The Talbot Press, 1969,
58-69.

Stanley, David and Brown, Raymond. "Aspects of New Testament
Thought," in R. Brown, J. Fitzmyer, and R. Murphy eds.
The Jerome Biblical Commentary. Englewood Cliffs, New
Jersey: Prentice-Hall, Inc., 1968, Section 78, 768-799.

Periodicals

Brown, Raymond E. "Second Thoughts on the Dead Sea Scrolls and the
New Testament," The Expository Times, October, 1966, LXXVII,
19-23.

Brownlee, William H. "John the Baptist in the New Light of Ancient
Scrolls," Interpretation, 1955, 9, 71-90.

Collins, Berkeley, "The Sacrament of Baptism in the New Testament," *The Expository Times*, 1915, XXVII, 36-39.

Cullmann, Oscar. "The Significance of the Qumran Texts for Research into the Beginnings of Christianity," *Journal of Biblical Literature*, 1955, LXXIV, 213-226.

Driver, Geoffrey. "Mythology of Qumran," *Jewish Quarterly Review*, April, 1958, LXI, 241-281.

Finkelstein, Louis. "The Institution of Baptism in Judaism for Proselytes," *Journal of Biblical Literature*, 1933, LII, 203-211.

Funk, Robert. "The Wilderness," *Journal of Biblical Literature*, 1959, 78, 205-214..

Heron, John. "The Theology of Baptism," *Scottish Journal of Theology*, 1955, 8, 36-63.

Higgins, A. G. M. P. "A Few Thoughts on the Dead Sea Scrolls," *Modern Churchmen*, January, 1970, 13, 198-201.

Jeremias, Joachim. "The Theological Significance of the Dead Sea Scrolls," *Concordia Theological Monthly*, September, 1968, 39, 557-571.

McCown, C. C. "The Scene of John's Ministry and Its Relation to the Purpose and Outcome of His Mission," *Journal of Biblical Literature*, LIX, 113-131.

Mowry, Lucretta. "The Dead Sea Scrolls and the Background for the Gospel of John," *The Biblical Archaeologist*, December, 1954, XVII, 78-97.

Pryke, John E. "John the Baptist and the Qumran Community," *Revue de Qumran*, April, 1964, 4, 483-496.

Robinson, John A. "The Baptism of John and the Qumran Community," *Harvard Theological Studies*, 1957, 50, 157-191.

Rowley, H. H. "The Qumran Sect and Christian Origins," *Bulletin of the John Ryland's Library*, 1961-1962, XLIV, 141-145.

Rowley, H. H. "The Origin and Meaning of Baptism," Baptist
    Quarterly, XI, 309-320, 1942-1945.

Sutcliffe, Edmund F. "Baptism and Baptismal Rites at Qumran,"
    Heythrop Journal, 1960, I, 179-188.

Sutcliffe, Edmund F. "Sacred Meals at Qumran?" Heythrop Journal
    1960, I, 48-65.

Torrance, Thomas F. "Aspects of Baptism in the New Testament,"
    Theologische Zeitschrift, July-August, 1958, 14, 241-260.

Torrance, Thomas F. "The Origins of Baptism," Scottish Journal
    of Theology, July, 1958, XI, 158-171.

Zeitlin, Solomon. "The Dead Sea Scrolls: A Travesty on
    Scholarship," Jewish Quarterly Review, 1956-1957, XLVII, 1-3, 6.

Zeitlin, Solomon. "The Hebrew Scrolls and the Status of Biblical
    Scholarship," Jewish Quarterly Review, 1951, 42, 133-192.

Zeitlin, Solomon. "A Note on Baptism for Proselytes," Journal
    of Biblical Literature, 1933, LII, 56-60.